T0252428

Appcelerator Titanium:
Up and Running

John Anderson

O'REILLY®

Beijing · Cambridge · Farnham · Köln · Sebastopol · Tokyo

Appcelerator Titanium: Up and Running

by John Anderson

Copyright © 2013 John Anderson. All rights reserved.

Printed in the United States of America.

Published by O'Reilly Media, Inc., 1005 Gravenstein Highway North, Sebastopol, CA 95472.

O'Reilly books may be purchased for educational, business, or sales promotional use. Online editions are also available for most titles (*http://my.safaribooksonline.com*). For more information, contact our corporate/institutional sales department: 800-998-9938 or *corporate@oreilly.com*.

Editors: Andy Oram and Mike Hendrickson
Production Editor: Kara Ebrahim
Proofreader: Kara Ebrahim

Cover Designer: Randy Comer
Interior Designer: David Futato
Illustrator: Rebecca Demarest

March 2013:   First Edition

Revision History for the First Edition:

2013-03-08:   First release

See *http://oreilly.com/catalog/errata.csp?isbn=9781449329556* for release details.

ISBN: 978-1-449-32955-6

[LSI]

Table of Contents

Preface

Introduction

Titanium allows you to create mobile applications on multiple platforms from a single codebase using native UI components. This allows you to create applications that perform well, and look great across multiple operating systems.

Conventions Used in This Book

The following typographical conventions are used in this book:

Italic
> Indicates new terms, URLs, email addresses, filenames, and file extensions.

`Constant width`
> Used for program listings, as well as within paragraphs to refer to program elements such as variable or function names, databases, data types, environment variables, statements, and keywords.

`Constant width bold`
> Shows commands or other text that should be typed literally by the user.

`Constant width italic`
> Shows text that should be replaced with user-supplied values or by values determined by context.

 This icon signifies a tip, suggestion, or general note.

This icon indicates a warning or caution.

Using Code Examples

This book is here to help you get your job done. In general, if this book includes code examples, you may use the code in your programs and documentation. You do not need to contact us for permission unless you're reproducing a significant portion of the code. For example, writing a program that uses several chunks of code from this book does not require permission. Selling or distributing a CD-ROM of examples from O'Reilly books does require permission. Answering a question by citing this book and quoting example code does not require permission. Incorporating a significant amount of example code from this book into your product's documentation does require permission.

We appreciate, but do not require, attribution. An attribution usually includes the title, author, publisher, and ISBN. For example: "*Appcelerator Titanium: Up and Running* by John Anderson (O'Reilly). Copyright 2013 John Anderson, 978-1-449-32955-6."

If you feel your use of code examples falls outside fair use or the permission given above, feel free to contact us at *permissions@oreilly.com*.

Safari® Books Online

 Safari Books Online (*www.safaribooksonline.com*) is an on-demand digital library that delivers expert content in both book and video form from the world's leading authors in technology and business.

Technology professionals, software developers, web designers, and business and creative professionals use Safari Books Online as their primary resource for research, problem solving, learning, and certification training.

Safari Books Online offers a range of product mixes and pricing programs for organizations, government agencies, and individuals. Subscribers have access to thousands of books, training videos, and prepublication manuscripts in one fully searchable database from publishers like O'Reilly Media, Prentice Hall Professional, Addison-Wesley Professional, Microsoft Press, Sams, Que, Peachpit Press, Focal Press, Cisco Press, John Wiley & Sons, Syngress, Morgan Kaufmann, IBM Redbooks, Packt, Adobe Press, FT Press, Apress, Manning, New Riders, McGraw-Hill, Jones & Bartlett, Course Technology, and dozens more. For more information about Safari Books Online, please visit us online.

How to Contact Us

Please address comments and questions concerning this book to the publisher:

O'Reilly Media, Inc.
1005 Gravenstein Highway North
Sebastopol, CA 95472
800-998-9938 (in the United States or Canada)
707-829-0515 (international or local)
707-829-0104 (fax)

We have a web page for this book, where we list errata, examples, and any additional information. You can access this page at *http://oreil.ly/app-titanium*.

To comment or ask technical questions about this book, send email to *bookques tions@oreilly.com*.

For more information about our books, courses, conferences, and news, see our website at *http://www.oreilly.com*.

Find us on Facebook: *http://facebook.com/oreilly*

Follow us on Twitter: *http://twitter.com/oreillymedia*

Watch us on YouTube: *http://www.youtube.com/oreillymedia*

Acknowledgments

Thanks to everyone who helped out with the book. It's far better than I would have been able to do on my own.

Thanks to John Plebanski, Maximiliano Firtman, Sanjeev Dhavala, and Michal F. Collins III for their insights into the book during its growth. Thanks to Andy at O'Reilly for caring about this book as much as I did and helping me to make the best book possible.

Thanks to Appcelerator for making Titanium to bring back the fun into programming again. When you can focus on the functionality of a mobile app, without having to worry as much about the nitty-gritty details, it's always more fun and more of a joy to do.

Most importantly, thanks to my loving wife Lisa and the rest of the family for giving me the time away from them to work on this. Without them to share the end result, the pursuit of the book would mean nothing.

CHAPTER 1

The Benefits of Titanium

If you're reading this book, you probably want to know more about Titanium, so let's do a quick overview to make sure we're all starting on the same page.

Titanium is a product by a company called Appcelerator that allows you to build mobile apps in JavaScript and compile it out to native apps for iOS, Android, and BlackBerry. Although BlackBerry support does exist, it's not nearly as mature or robust as iOS and Android. However, if you absolutely must have BlackBerry versions of your app, it's good to know that it's there.

Although Titanium does use JavaScript, it's very, very important to note that you're not building your apps using HTML5 or CSS3, just JavaScript. With a web page, you modify CSS properties to modify the look and feel of the objects. But if you want to change the appearance of a button in Titanium, you modify parameters on the button to change its look and feel. The concepts are similar, but good to know that CSS isn't used at all with Titanium. When you compile your Titanium app to iOS or Android, the Titanium "engine" processes your JavaScript and then builds an appropriate native project for the platform that you're building for.

For iOS, this means that an actual Xcode project is created and then compiled using Apple's compiler, so that you end up with a native .IPA that you can deploy to a device, or Apple's App Store. It's a similar process with Android. A native Java mobile application is created and compiled using the Android compiler. The end application that is created is 100% native, using 100% native controls.

Even though Titanium makes use of the native SDKs for the different platforms it supports, you don't really need to know much about them other than how to get them installed on your development system. Once the SDKs are there you can almost forget about them since Titanium interacts with them behind the scenes for you.

Knowing JavaScript is of course a prerequisite to using Titanium. JavaScript is a pretty nice language for writing a mobile app. It has its own object-oriented model, with methods and properties. When you are using JavaScript within a web page, you work with DOM objects and other objects exposed by the web browser. When you are using JavaScript with Titanium, you work with the objects that Titanium provides via its API to build web apps.

So on a web page, you'll do something like create a div, add it to the body section of the current document, and set properties on the div via JavaScript. With Titanium, you'll create an object (such as a window or a button), set properties on that object, and call methods to open the window, or add the button to the window.

When to Use Titanium

There are many situations where it makes sense to use Titanium, but it's not always appropriate for a mobile app. I'll be the first to admit that there is no one-size-fits-all solution for just about anything in life, and mobile is no exception.

A carpenter has a toolbox with many tools at his disposal. When he's in a particular situation he understands the job that needs to be done, and selects an appropriate tool. The same thing goes for mobile development. There are multiple platforms to run mobile apps on and multiple tools that can be used to build those apps. Only after taking the following into account can you intelligently make a good tool selection:

1. What is the functionality of this app?
2. Who is going to be using the app?
3. How is the app going to be distributed?
4. How many platforms will the app need to run on?

When Titanium Makes Sense

When choosing a tool to develop mobile apps, it's important to know why you're using that tool versus something else. When you want to drive a nail into a piece of wood, you choose a hammer because it's designed for that task. If the task at hand was to turn a screw into a piece of wood, a hammer would be a very bad tool choice. However, if you didn't know about a screwdriver, or the advantages it would bring to the problem at hand (getting a nail into the piece of wood), you could mistakenly use a hammer. As the old phrase goes, "When all you have is a hammer, everything in the world looks like a nail."

Choosing a tool for mobile development is similar. There are multiple solutions on the market, each with their own pros and cons. The key to making an informed decision about what tool to use is knowing the pros and cons of each particular tool and using that as a guide for which one to use for a particular problem.

There are several good reasons to use Titanium. The most obvious reason is that you can develop your app in JavaScript and then compile it out to native apps on multiple platforms. Right now the most obvious and popular platforms that Titanium supports is iOS and Android. They do have a version for BlackBerry, which was updated in the summer of 2011 with many great enhancements.

The Mobile Web Platform

Mobile Web is a recent feature added to the Titanium Framework to make it as easy to create mobile web applications. These run in web browsers and therefore allow you to run your app on a device that isn't natively supported by Titanium. Mobile Web is in beta now, which means that it still probably has its share of warts, but it's worth keeping an eye on.

What you'll end up with is a JavaScript/CSS/HTML5 app that runs pretty much like something that you'd see developed to run inside of PhoneGap, but it will be a mobile app. This will be a handy ability to have, since right now there is no low-cost development environment that can do this.

If Appcelerator does it right, this should make it just as easy to produce an HTML5 mobile version of an app as it is to create a native app. This will help round out their product offering so that it can address both native apps and mobile web apps from a single code base.

The hidden "gotchas" will be found in the fact that Titanium was started as a toolkit to build native apps running on mobile devices. So, there will be times when you might be able to do something in an API that simply can't be translated into a mobile app, such as accessing contacts, or taking a picture. You can certainly do things like that with the PhoneGap/Cordova APIs, but then we're not talking about a web app.

What this means is that, even though you'll be able to generate a mobile web app from the same codebase as a native app, functionality of the native app may be constrained by the requirement that one of your build targets is a mobile web app. For example, if you want to write to the local filesystem in your native app, this won't translate into a web app. So you'll either need to do things differently based on the platform you're running on, or just not allow that functionality in the app at all.

Cross-Platform Compatibility

Since Titanium allows you to create apps on three platforms, it makes a lot of sense to use Titanium to achieve some cross-platform results. But before we talk about how compatible Titanium's API is between iOS and Android, let's talk about how cross-platform compatible it *can* be.

There are plenty of differences between iOS and Android, but there are plenty of similarities too. Android seems to have "followed Apple's lead" with much of its design, including the home screen, title bar, etc. I'm sure Apple is not too happy about this, but it makes it good for developers that the screen aspect ratio is the same, and that many of the UI elements (tables, table rows, switches, sliders, etc.) exist in both platforms.

 Windows 8 support will be added to Titanium in the second half of 2013, according to an announcement released by Appcelerator in February of that year. This will allow you to also create apps for both Windows RT and Windows Phone. There is also a very preliminary version of Titanium that allows you to create apps for the BlackBerry Z10.

The recent ruling in the Apple/Samsung lawsuit shows that Android did borrow a concept or two from Apple's design. What does this mean for the future of Android? It's hard to say, but this ruling is certainly a good thing for Apple. Does is mean the death of Android? I doubt it. Does it mean higher prices as Android manufacturers pay Apple a licensing fee? Maybe. With this ruling in mind, Windows 8 may seem like a more viable option for mobile apps.

I always like to try to figure out what a company is going to be doing in 6 months by seeing who they are hiring now. I recently saw a job posting on Appcelerator's site for a "Windows 8 Developer - Mobile Technology." I'm sure that Windows 8 has always been on Appcelerator's corporate mind as a platform that could be worth developing for, at some point. Apple's ruling in court may help accelerate Appcelerator's development of Windows 8 as a new platform in the Titanium family.

 Be careful about taking a "lowest common denominator" approach when coming up with a cross-platform app. You'll just end up with an app that doesn't work great on any platform.

Once you start talking about the Android platform, the next thing to examine is the number of hardware devices that the Android Platform runs on. One huge difference about Apple and other software companies is their feelings about having their software run on hardware made by third parties. Apple tried licensing in the past and it didn't seem to work out well for them. They are now strictly in the mode of controlling every aspect of the user experience, and that includes being the only manufacturer of the hardware that iOS runs on. This does have a huge positive impact on the user experience. Apple hardware has always been top-notch and just gets better with each new release.

A similarly huge side benefit for Apple developers is that by owning maybe five pieces of hardware, they can test their app on the actual hardware their users will be using.

With perhaps two or three iPhones, a couple iPads, and an iPod touch (I just borrow my kids to test apps on), a developer can make sure the app will perform well on the devices.

More importantly, the developer can rest assured that the hardware used to test on represents 95% or more of the 90+ million users that might be running her app. This tight control follows over onto the software side as well, helping the developer know that on hardware *X* running software version *y*, things will go well. Just a few pieces of hardware, and a few different OS versions to test on…nice.

The biggest hurdle to overcome when developing for Android is the huge segmentation of different hardware platforms. This makes it hard to ensure your app will run well on all devices. Don't underestimate the time you have to spend on testing on various Android hardware. Sometimes it's good to try to select a subset of the top Android models focus on making it work well for the 80% or 90% of the most-used devices.

OK, now that we've set the stage, let's talk about Titanium's cross-platform API. I think that the API differences can be put into two categories: functional/UI-related and OS-related. For instance, activities are a big part of Android that don't really have a corresponding part in iOS.

Titanium has pretty effectively isolated the different APIs and put them in their own namespaces, which is good. In fact, with the new release, they seem to have made things a little more granular between iOS and Android, such as `Ti.UI.createTabbedBar` becoming `Ti.UI.iOS.createTabbedBar`, indicating that this is clearly an iOS object and not something shared between iOS and Android.

Later on in, I'll talk about a compatibility layer that I have come up with after working on several Titanium projects and wanting to find some way to reduce the number of lines of code that I need to write to do a single task, such as writing data to a file. A compatibility layer is an API, either home-grown or developed by someone else, that runs on top of the standard API and makes calls to it internally. This is a great way to handle the differences between platforms and devices. My own compatibility layer is located in my own namespace (TiCL), where I store functions that help even out the differences between iOS and Android and some simple convenience functions.

Using Titanium for Just One Platform

Although one of Titanium's strengths is obviously generating native apps for multiple platforms from a single JavaScript code base, it also makes sense to use Titanium even if just one of these OS's is going to be used. Titanium offers plenty of other value besides cross-platform development.

Titanium allows you to create mobile apps using JavaScript. This is without a doubt the biggest advantage that Titanium brings. Its ability to create mobile apps for multiple platforms just makes it that much more powerful. These benefits are independent of each other, meaning that even if you are going to deploy only to iOS, Titanium shouldn't be automatically ruled out. The value of making a mobile app in JavaScript still exists and should still be considered a tick in the "pro" column for Titanium.

Using Titanium allows you to write mobile apps without having to get into all the details of the platform you are deploying to. Without something like Titanium, there are many things you would need to come up to speed on to get even a basic app done. There are many memory management issues that you would need to deal with, making sure you only call Public APIs if you're going through the App Store, making sure you deallocate anything that you allocate, making sure your code is organized, etc. Another aspect is the relatively large learning curve of getting up to speed on Objective-C.

To help show exactly where Titanium helps bring value and increase productivity, here are the three steps that need to happen to learn and become proficient with a new programming language:

Learn the language
> This is where you learn the syntax of a new language.

Learn the API
> Just about any modern programming language has a namespace and API that you need to learn. There is usually a namespace that organizes the functions into a logical manner.

Gain experience
> After working with a particular language and learning the API for a particular platform, experience is still required. When you come across a situation that is similar to something you've done in the past, you can supply the solution quickly and efficiently.

When you learn a completely new language, such as Objective-C, you have a learning curve in all of these areas. There is a new language to learn, there is a new API to learn, and you don't really have any experience to draw upon.

Titanium lets anyone with JavaScript skills leverage them to quickly create mobile apps. You have already gone through the first and third areas mentioned earlier: you already know the language, and there is experience using it that you can draw upon. It is mainly learning the API where the time is spent in getting up to speed with Titanium.

When Titanium Doesn't Make Sense

I think that the most situations where Titanium doesn't make sense is where people confuse the differences between PhoneGap and Titanium. Looking at the community forums, sometimes people will begin asking questions like "How do I a create a tableview in a web view?" That line of questioning seems that Titanium is more like PhoneGap, which is HTML-based for the UI elements. Titanium doesn't make a lot of sense if what you're trying to do is to create an HTML-based "hybrid" app. Having Titanium at your disposal, I would go the extra mile and learn the API and see how it does making an app that uses native controls.

 If, during a Titanium project, you find yourself dropping in a Web View and starting to build your app in HTML5, CSS, and JavaScript, it's time to ask yourself why you're using Titanium.

I've been down the PhoneGap route. What I found is that I was spending a lot of time trying to come up with just the right HTML5/CSS to duplicate UI controls that already exist. I actually extended PhoneGap to allow me to create native controls that weren't available out of the box. That was actually easier than trying to recreate those controls in HTML5 and keep the UX as smooth and fluid as in native iOS.

Now don't get me wrong: I'm not saying don't use PhoneGap. Just use it where it makes sense, or where you can leverage the strengths that it brings to the party. PhoneGap goes across the most number of mobile platforms, and provides some access to native functionality, but it doesn't go as deep as Titanium, especially along the lines of UI components. Titanium provides support on a smaller number of platforms, but goes much deeper providing access to functionality on those platforms (see Figure 1-1 for a visual representation of the difference).

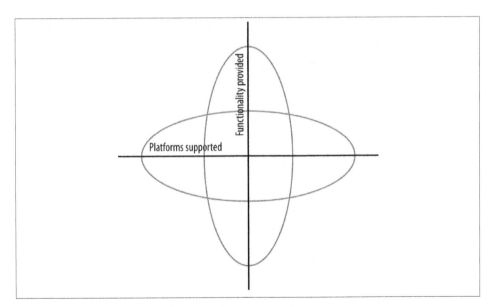

Figure 1-1. Platforms versus functionality supported

So, if you've got your heart set on doing all the UI/UX in HTML5, use PhoneGap. If you don't mind learning a few more API calls, I think you'll be pleasantly surprised with what you can do in Titanium.

Mobile Landscape

Although this book is about Appcelerator's Titanium, I wanted to add a little information about similar products in the mobile space. As they say, everything is good or bad by comparison. No tool is right in every situation. Hopefully, by putting Titanium side by side with some other tools, you'll see the value Titanium brings.

PhoneGap

PhoneGap is a nice tool that allows you to put a mobile website into an "app wrapper" that runs on a mobile device on many different platforms. It also lets you access some native functionality of the device. It allows you to do this across a wide variety of mobile devices. PhoneGap doesn't provide as much functionality as other products, especially in the UI area, but it covers many platforms and is quite powerful. Their API gives you access to many of the more "functional" areas of a mobile device, such as GPS, filesystem, device info, calendar info, accelerometer, etc. This gives you access to more areas of the device than you can get with a web application, even using HTML5.

The trade-off in using PhoneGap is that you have no access to familiar, native controls. You'll have to use HTML5, CSS, and JavaScript to make your own user interface. The challenge then becomes having a UI that is quick and responsive across many different devices, screen sizes, and screen densities. Using responsive design and some common sense CSS, such as using lots of relative sizes and resolution-independent units of measure (such as ems), can make your cross platform app work well across the wide diversity of devices that it will encounter.

Another differentiator for PhoneGap is the PhoneGap build service. Using PhoneGap to create a web app wrapped into an app wrapper is a great way to make an app, but you still need native SDKs and compilers to actually compile the app on different platforms. PhoneGap helps you out there with their build service. You upload the code for your website to PhoneGap's cloud-based service, which builds a native app and lets you download it.

If you've gone through the headaches of installing and configuring mobile SDKs for multiple platforms, you'll love the new service. If you haven't gone through those headaches, you'll still love it, maybe just a little less. Keep in mind that although PhoneGap does produce a native app, all the code is executed in JavaScript through a Chrome-less web browser. This provides another layer that the code has to go through, which will affect performance to a degree.

Sencha Touch

Sencha Touch is a nice framework that allows you to create mobile apps with a fantastic look and feel, especially for iOS devices. Sencha Touch is a JavaScript-based framework with tons of objects that you can use with minimal effort and ramp-up time. Since it's 100% JavaScript, it still has to run through a web browser, and goes through that same layer as PhoneGap.

Sencha Touch's differentiator is that it has a large library of JavaScript objects that you can use with a standard JavaScript syntax. Sencha Touch doesn't provide any access to native features of a device, except those that you could get at using HTML5.

This framework by Sencha is also very object oriented and allows you to create your own objects based on its built-in objects. In fact, there are a few key base objects, such as views, buttons, and labels, that many of the other built-in objects simply extend. This gives their objects a bit more reliability, as there are fewer unique moving parts involved in each object you end up using.

Sencha Touch and PhoneGap make a good team. Recent releases of Sencha Touch let you package your Sencha Touch app as a native app without involving PhoneGap. I believe, however, in using products that are based on the core competencies of a company. PhoneGap's main purpose is providing access to features of a native device, but not much on the UI side. Sencha Touch helps you make killer UIs, but is totally web-based. Using these two products together will allow you to get the benefits of each.

jQuery Mobile

Leveraging the popularity of jQuery, jQuery Mobile brings all the power and familiarity of jQuery to mobile development. jQuery Mobile allows you to quickly get a mobile app up and running with a nice-looking UI and advanced functionality such as form validation very easily.

Using the `data-role` attribute heavily, jQuery Mobile allows you to easily assign functionality to traditional HTML components without having to worry about many of the "lower-level" details such as padding and margins and focus on the functionality of your app.

Being able to write and use plug-ins has always been a big feature in jQuery, which is of course present in jQuery Mobile. This allows you to make use of mobile-focused components written by others, such as Photo Albums, mobile Drag and Drop, Google Map functionality, Date Pickers, Action Sheet-like components and many others.

jQuery Mobile is a nice middle ground between something like jQTouch, which is focused on giving you many CSS classes to make your mobile app look great, and something like Sencha Touch. Sencha Touch is much more programmer-oriented and has a steeper learning curve than something like jQuery Mobile. jQuery Mobile makes it easy to use the power of programming yet still do your mobile development within the familiar confines of divs.

jQTouch

jQTouch, a library based on the extremely popular jQuery library, is similar to Sencha Touch in that it is totally web-based. When you create an app with jQTouch, you have to think about your layout in terms of divs and uls and other such HTML markup. Sencha Touch, in contrast, allows you to think in terms of Toolbars and Tabs.

Still, if you're familiar with HTML and JavaScript, jQTouch allows you to get up to speed making apps pretty quickly, especially if you're familiar with jQuery. The examples included get you off to a quick start. Once you start seeing how to transform a list of uls into an iOS-looking tableview, you'll quickly be mobile.

This lower ramp-up speed comes at the expense of not having nearly as robust of an environment in which to work, and not as many objects at your disposal. For example, Sencha Touch helps not only in the UI arena, but with objects that help you retrieve and process data from web services. With jQTouch, if it's not already included in HTML5/CSS3/JavaScript or jQuery, you're on your own.

PhoneGap and jQTouch play well together as well, if you want your jQTouch app in the App Store, or Android Marketplace. Although not quite as sophisticated as Sencha Touch, jQTouch is a good way to get started in mobile development or to whip up a quick proof of concept.

MonoTouch

MonoTouch is a product that, on the surface, seems fairly similar to Titanium in that it allows you to build a native app using a language other than what the native compiler uses. Titanium allows you to build your app in JavaScript and compile for different platforms. MonoTouch does the same thing for C#/.NET technologies.

Deciding between Titanium and MonoTouch will basically boil down deciding which language you want, and the direction your company takes. Appcelerator, in an effort to add value to their core product, is adding peripheral products and services to their "ecosystem." These products and services add value to the Titanium developer and help in getting more sophisticated apps up and running quickly. I don't see Xamarin adding such products and services to help the MonoTouch developers.

Another key variable in the equation is your development staff. It's good to think about getting your development staff up and running quickly using a technology they are comfortable with. It's also just as important to think about how much it will cost to replace them when they leave for greener pastures. If you hang your hat on a product that is based on C#/.NET, you'll have no choice but to hire that level of developer when you need to replace someone. If you use a product based on JavaScript, you'll need to replace someone at that level.

Where's the GUI?

After you start using Titanium, one of the questions that will probably come up is "Where is the GUI (Graphical User Interface) used to design the screen layouts?" That's a very valid question and the bottom line is that there simply isn't one...yet. There are some third-party products available that allow you to get around this to some extent.

Does that mean that you shouldn't use Titanium since there isn't a polished GUI screen editor in place? That's entirely up to you. Many programmers (myself included) sometimes prefer to create user screens via code instead of a GUI-based drag and drop interface. Others like the ease of just dropping some controls onto a screen and set some properties via drop-downs, etc.

It boils down to part personal preference and part looking at the overall value proposition of Titanium. Titanium lets you develop cross-platform apps with JavaScript. That allows you to create iOS apps without necessarily knowing Objective-C and the iOS API, and create Android apps without having to know Java and the Android API. If you're making a pros and cons list, then you've got two pretty serious checkmarks in the pros section and a check in the cons section due to the lack of a GUI-based screen editor.

Looking at some examples, even on Apple's site about UI programming, many times you'll see instructions on how to do it via Xcode and Interface Builder (Xcode's GUI screen editor) and a section immediately after on how to do the same UI layout in code. Point being, there are some who prefer using GUI editors, and some who prefer doing the layout in code.

Death of Xcode and ADK?

With a big part of the value proposition of Titanium being able to write cross-platform apps using JavaScript, does this mean that Xcode and Android Development Kit will become endangered species? The short and long answer is no. This is a question that I've heard from time to time and the question being asked is actually the first thing to notice.

When looking at new tools or different tools, you need to have the right mindset. Since mobile is still relatively new and young, there are lots of different tools coming out in the mobile space. Each one has lots of promises and is positioning itself to be the "next big thing."

It's important to remember that there is no one tool that will do everything. Even though tools like Titanium allow you to write cross-platform apps, it's not necessarily meant to replace Xcode altogether. Granted, the goal would be that something like Titanium would allow you to develop, say, 70% to 80% of your apps. If you are working at a company that has chosen to embrace Titanium, this could easily jump to 100%. If you're working at a company that does a wide variety of apps, something like 70% would be a reasonable target.

Here's another way of looking at this situation: let's say a company has some talented Objective-C developers who they use to make high performance iOS apps. If the company wants to create more apps, perhaps ones that are less high-performance oriented, they can either try to get expensive Objective-C resources or look at other ways of developing apps.

Titanium allows a company such as this to supplement their existing mobile development staff with other JavaScript-based developers to help produce apps that might not have extreme performance requirements. The Titanium developers can then build many apps that are more functional-based than performance-based, as businesses start wanting more and more mobile apps to simply extend their information to their workforce. This doesn't require a deep knowledge of iOS or Android and allows JavaScript developers to create these apps.

For more performance-oriented apps, such as games, you have good reasons to put hardcore iOS developers on the project. The financials would follow suit as well. The higher-priced iOS developers can be expected to create apps that companies would charge more for. Titanium developers would create apps that are lower cost to the end client.

The important thing to remember is there is no one-size-fits-all solution. There is no one tool that will fit all your needs, mobile or otherwise. The only way to successfully use tools such as Titanium, and Xcode and Android tools, is to know the strengths and weaknesses of each one and know when to use which tool.

Much like a golfer who has a number of clubs at his disposal, a developer has to understand the tools at his disposal and when to use each one. Trouble is, many developers don't properly understand the tools available to them and they sometimes make the wrong choice. Then, halfway through a project, it's discovered that the wrong tool is being used and it needs to be twisted into doing something it wasn't really designed for.

The intent of this book is to show you the strengths and weaknesses of Titanium and help you understand when to use it, and when it doesn't make sense to use it. Hopefully it will help you to put an extra club or two in your bag and know when to use them.

Pricing and Support

Like any robust software package, Titanium offers different pricing options. The good news is that you can use it for free, put apps into the App Store and Google Play for free, and maintain and update those apps for free. The bottom line is that you can try out and use Titanium for free. There is also a free level of Appcelerator Cloud Services that allows you to try these features as well. The limits on these have also been bumped up very recently (as of the writing of this book) to give you more room to experiment with them.

Outside of the Titanium SDK and Titanium Studio, the next thing that developers will be interested in are the Cloud Services that Appcelerator has to offer. As of this writing, at the free level, you can send 5,000,000 push notifications, make 5,000,000 API calls, use up to 20 GB of storage, and send 100,000 emails. You also have the ability to log 1,000,000 analytic events from your app. This is certainly more than enough to play around with what Appcelerator has to offer without spending a dime. When you start going over those limits, you'll have to start paying.

But, as the saying goes, "You get what you pay for." Don't look for much hand-holding or support when you're making use of the free levels of Titanium. That's not to say you're not without any help. There has always been a great community Q&A forum on Appcelerator's website. The biggest caveat in using this resource is to keep in mind the dates that issues were logged. There are issues in the forum that are years old and may not even be relevant, such as a bug report that may have been fixed now. That being said, there is a wealth of small examples and starters to help newcomers to Titanium find their way around.

Appcelerator offers additional levels of paid support, for which you pay on an annual basis. Most levels of support are targeted at Enterprise Developers. In addition to better response time for your support questions, you have access to Titanium components that are not available to users of the free versions. Of course everyone wants as much as possible for free, but as developers we also have to see the value of paid support. There are different variables involved in that pricing, so it's impossible to quote any numbers here.

You can get far using Titanium for free, but you need to do a little more legwork on your own, and be able to troubleshoot your own issues. I, for one, am glad that there are options to use Titanium for free, in return for putting a little "sweat equity" into your project. This is a great way to get your feet wet seeing how Titanium works, without draining your wallet.

CHAPTER 2

Getting Set Up to Use Titanium

Because Titanium creates a native project for whatever platform you are targeting from JavaScript code, you need to have the native compilers installed for whichever platforms you want to run the app on. This chapter explains your options.

Selecting a Development Environment

If you want to do iOS development, you'll need to get a Mac. When I first got into mobile development, and wanted to get my feet wet while investing the least amount of money, I bought a Mac Mini. It worked very well for iPhone development.

Android development is more platform-agnostic, but you'll want to get something with plenty of horsepower. Compiling for Android is more CPU intensive than compiling for iOS, so if a decent amount of your work will be for Android, think about getting something like a MacBook Pro. The current lineup of MacBook Pro laptops are a great combination of portability and power.

 Depending on what kind of environment you'll be working in, seriously consider a laptop. Nothing beats being able to pick up your development environment for a quick demo or a trip to the local Starbucks.

And the importance of memory is as true as ever. Additional memory for Mac or Windows will help speed up things. I expanded my MacBook Pro with memory bought from Amazon and it worked fine. Don't think that low-cost memory is cheap or will not work. But as always, your results may vary.

Recent changes to the Titanium engine for Android makes it possible to make changes to the *.js* files in your Android project, restart the app in the simulator, and see your changes reflected when you tap on the app icon in the Android simulator. This is a huge time saver over earlier Titanium versions, where any change to a *.js* file would require a full recompile taking literally 60 seconds or more. Talk about painful programming!

If you want to be a three-headed Hydra and develop apps for iOS, Android, and BlackBerry, accept the idea that you're going to need two development machines, or use something like Parallels on your Mac (which is actually quite effective). Right now, the BlackBerry SDK runs only on Windows, so you'll need that environment at your disposal in either a virtualized or physical state.

Bear in mind, if you do tread into the BlackBerry side of development, this side of Titanium is less advanced than the iOS and Android versions. Programming on BlackBerry in any form is not an incredibly pleasant experience, and this translates over into Titanium as well. That being said, Appcelerator has done a good job of allowing Titanium apps access to this platform.

Setting Up Your Native SDKs

The iOS development environment, Xcode, is fairly easy to get installed. Once you sign up as an Apple Developer, just load up the Mac App Store and "purchase" iOS 5.0 (it's free) for Xcode. Then go get a cup of coffee, or take a break and get some exercise depending on your download speed, as the package is about 4.5 GB in size. But, it's very easy to install after that, so your patience will be rewarded.

 OS X's update with Lion and Xcode 4.2 made setting up your Mac easier than ever. Start up your Mac and go to the App Store. There is an Xcode 4.2 "app" that installs into your environment with literally two or three clicks. Now the biggest problem you'll have is deciding which movie to watch while it's downloading.

Although installing the Android SDK (or ADK, Android Development Kit) isn't really all that hard, it's a little more involved than the iOS one. And that's to be expected. Apple is continually looking for ways to make the user experience less and less painful. Android seems to fall into the PC mentality, where users are expected to be able to do more of the work. Luckily, it's not that much more. Although there are some pain points you just can't get around (particularly the task of provisioning profiles), the Android team tries to make things as easy as possible.

The Android documentation advises installing Eclipse before you download the SDK. I didn't have it installed when I installed the Android SDK and I haven't had any issues. It's okay to just skip over any references to Eclipse when you're setting up your Android SDK. If you're going to be using Titanium, then you'll need to install Titanium Studio and use some of its basic features. If you don't want to use it for your main text editor, that's fine, but you'll need to pop in and out of it to run your code in a simulator, etc.

Install the Android SDK from Android's developer site, choosing the appropriate version for your operating system (Figure 2-1). When you click on your link and the download starts, don't be fooled by how quickly it comes down. Although it's more than a bare bones installer, it doesn't have the majority of the components that you'll need to do anything. When you run the installer, it's a good idea not to change any of the defaults.

Figure 2-1. Android SDK download page

It's a good idea not to change any of the defaults. Titanium expects it to be installed in the default location. If you install the SDK in another location, you'll need to tell Titanium Studio, during its own installation, where the Android SDK is. This will just save you time and frustration later on when you need to let Titanium know where you installed it if it's in a custom location.

Getting the Android SDK running is a bit time consuming. After you get the base SDK downloaded and running, you'll have the opportunity to download "optional" extras that aren't so optional for some real world development. You can download the SDK modules for the various Android versions that you want to develop for.

Part of installing the Android SDK will force you to install an appropriate version of Java. Don't think that you need to install a version of Java with all the bells and whistles. Getting the most lightweight version of Java that will support the project you want to build is the best way to go. You can always install a more robust version later if you find that you need features that aren't present.

Here, the main decision you'll need to make is what versions of the Android SDK you want to download. You can download more than one if you want to test on multiple APIs. Version 4.0 is currently new whereas 1.6 is quite old. Current stats in the Android Marketplace are shown in Figure 2-2. This is one of my most widely installed apps, so it's a good yardstick to see what APIs people are running out there. Checking them can help you decide what APIs to support. As you can see, at the time of writing, 2.1, 2.2, and 2.3 take the greatest share of the users.

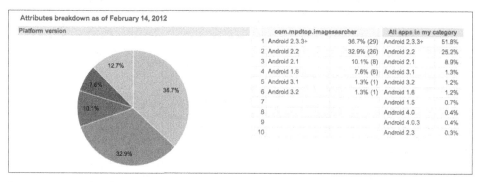

Figure 2-2. Android versions in current use

If you want to do BlackBerry development, get ready for more of an uphill battle. Its SDK is harder to install than the others. iOS and Android have much more autonomous installs, where it's almost as simple as "click it and forget it." BlackBerry has more steps to follow and finding documentation about those steps is harder.

Other Hardware Prerequisites

As I've mentioned, requirements for your computer are modest when doing mobile development. But there are some other useful considerations.

External Displays

The 13-inch MacBook Pro is small and compact, sitting in my lap nicely while I'm commuting on the train, and has a nice entry level price. Unfortunately, I'd like to have better screen resolution. So when I'm at home working, I hook up an external keyboard (either wireless or wired), along with my Bluetooth Magic Mouse of course, and a nice external display. It's amazing how much more productive you can be with a wide-screen LCD and an external keyboard (Figure 2-3). It gives you room for a large editing and debugging window, along with space for Android and iOS simulators running at the same time. For me, this is the best of both worlds: a nice productive environment when

I'm working at my desk, with the ability to take my development environment on the road.

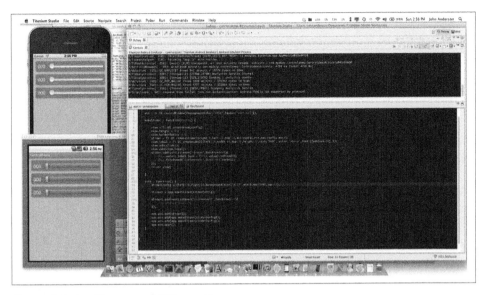

Figure 2-3. A wide-screen LCD monitor

The second screen also comes in handy. My typical development environment uses the large LCD screen for Titanium Studio, with reference material docked in the laptop's LCD screen. I have plenty of room on the wide-screen display for a large dock and the reference material is handy all the time.

You don't have to go nuts to get some productivity boosts. Although the Thunderbolt display is beautiful and provides a little extra real estate, much lower-cost displays work very well too. And with the money you save, you can max out your memory, get a MacBook Air, or just take a nice trip somewhere.

CHAPTER 3

Titanium Studio

In this chapter we start to see what makes Titanium so useful and popular. When your app is created in Titanium, a native project is created for the platforms you want to target, and then your JavaScript is baked into the binary. Although many JavaScript commands invoke a native component, some code functions remain in JavaScript and are run by native JavaScript engines on each platform.

Titanium Studio is an Integrated Development Environment (IDE), offering a single interface with which to manage your Titanium projects. Every Titanium developer uses Titanium Studio to some extent, as you need it to run your apps in a simulator or on a device, and to send your apps to Apple's App Store and Android Marketplace.

Features of Titanium Studio

After you install Titanium and start it up, you'll see a screen like Figure 3-1.

We're not going to get into all the details of Titanium Studio right now, but I'll just give you a quick tour of some of the features that you'll need to use to get your first project off the ground.

Figure 3-1. Titanium Studio after starting up

Automatic Syntax Checking

Syntax errors are usually the most common type. It's all too easy to forget a required comma or semicolon. When I first started using Titanium, it was sometimes a tedious process to uncover these errors and work through them one at a time when running the app.

The Titanium Studio editor's automatic syntax checking alerts you to any syntax errors as you're typing. This allows you to make sure that you won't get simple syntax errors when you're running your app. It might sound like a minor advantage, but it rescues you from getting sucked into a "run, fix, run, fix" cycle with simple errors.

Autocomplete (Intellisense)

Any useful development environment is bound to have a complex API with lots of namespaces that you need to keep track of. In addition to that, depending on how you structure your own apps in JavaScript, you'll be introducing your own variables and namespaces for custom attributes. For instance, let's assume that this snippet represents how you have your app structured:

```
app = {
  var1:10,
  var2:10,
}
```

In Titanium Studio, as you start typing app.v, a pop-up appears showing that you have two variables called var1 and var2, and allows you to select one with a single keystroke (Figure 3-2). This makes it much easier to be productive while you're coding and not have to go back and forth in your code listing to see what variables and methods you've set up.

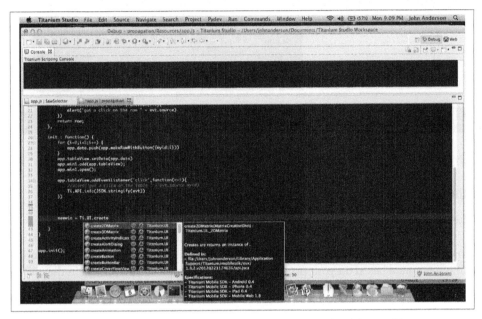

Figure 3-2. Titanium Studio helps you autocomplete methods and variables

Debugging

One of the more advanced and useful features of Titanium Studio is the ability to view debugging information that's a bit more on par with other development tools, such as setting breakpoints and watching the values of variables. Viewing multiple values as you run a program can be very helpful with larger apps that have many variables in use at any given time (see Figure 3-3).

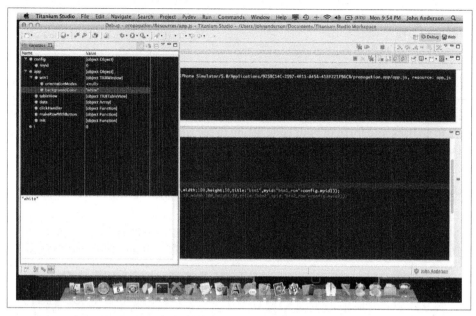

Figure 3-3. Titanium Studio allows you to inspect variables and attribute values

Building Your App

One of the features for which you *must* use Titanium is to build your app. This is where the magic happens. Titanium goes through your JavaScript code and builds up a native project, either iOS or Android, and compiles it. This is done by a complicated script that is generated based on your project settings. Titanium builds a project in the native environment you select and then uses native tools to compile your app into a native binary.

On the Android side, Titanium Studio helps you manage the Android simulator images that you are working with. Because the Android platform is run on so many different types of hardware and so many different types of display configurations, it's very helpful to be able to manage some different simulator images.

Titanium's Runtime Configuration helps you manage simulator-specific aspects on both iOS and Android. It's always best to use these tools inside of Titanium because they directly affect what happens when you run the app in an Android Simulator (Figure 3-4) and iOS simulator.

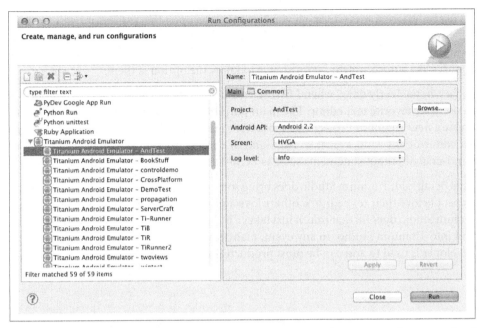

Figure 3-4. Titanium Studio allows you to manage the configurations of your Android virtual devices

Because Titanium works by kicking off external tools, it's important for Titanium to know how you want the simulator to act. With iOS, you can run the simulator in 4.3.5 mode or 5.1 mode. It's mandatory to tell Titanium Studio what you want so that it can start the correct simulator.

Titanium Studio and Other Text Editors

Programmers sometimes are hard pressed to give up their favorite text editor. Once you've got the function keys and key combos memorized, using a text editor that you know well can be a joy. Sometimes it's hard to know where the developer stops and where the computer begins.

Jumping into Titanium doesn't mean for a second that you have to give up a text editor that you know well and like using. When you run an app in a simulator or deploy it to an App Store or device, it all boils down to processing the text files that are in your Titanium project. Those text files can be modified by the text editor in Titanium Studio, or by a text editor of your choice. It won't have any effect on the end product. Using an external text editor doesn't short circuit anything in Titanium Studio that is needed by the compilation process.

To use an external text editor, all you need to do is open the *.js* files and edit them in whatever editor you'd like to use. There aren't any hidden files or indexes. that you need to update. You won't have the use of the debugging facilities at your disposal, or other features like autocomplete—it's just nice to know the option is there.

In fact, in the "early days" when I first started using Titanium, there was no choice but to use your favorite text editor. The main purpose of the Titanium UI was to help you create a new Titanium Project and show error messages while your app ran. There was no editor of any kind available. Any kind of variable tracing was done by executing hand-crafted output statements such as `Ti.API.info("var1 = " + var1)`.

That being said, Titanium Studio does bring some nice goodies to the table. Just as much as people love their text editors, others love a robust debugging environment, and Titanium Studio does fill that role. It just takes a little time to get out of your favorite editor and into Titanium Studio. In any event, many times the environment that a particular developer is used to and can be most productive in is usually the right choice.

CHAPTER 4

A Hello World App

We've talked a lot about building apps in the previous pages and now we're going to get our hands dirty getting something up and running.

Building Your First App

The first thing you do to create an app is to select New Project in Titanium Studio. This presents you with a New Project Wizard that will give you several options to select from (Figure 4-1). The options we'll focus on for this book will be the mobile ones.

 Titanium is capable of creating desktop apps as well as mobile apps. Desktop apps are out of the scope of this book, so we'll just focus on mobile apps for now. Appcelerator recently "spun off" the Desktop portion of Titanium into its own open source project. This allows Titanium Mobile to focus on the mobile side of cross platform apps.

Selecting the Titanium Mobile Project option gives you Figure 4-2. The fields you can fill out here are:

Project name
> This is a unique name you choose for your project.

Use default location
> Leaving this checked will cause Titanium Studio to generate and save your project files in the default location. Unless you have a good reason to store it somewhere else, leave this checked.

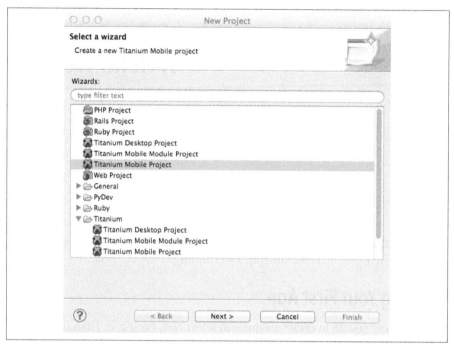

Figure 4-1. Titanium Studio New Project dialog

App Id

This is an important piece of information used when you upload your app to the App Store or Android Marketplace. When you start a new app in Apple's App Store, you have to set this field to the App ID that you are going to use, or have used. I've run into some issues when compiling for Android when there is an underscore in the App ID, so it's best just to use text characters in this field.

Company/Personal URL

This is a place to associate a URL with your app. Honestly, I've hardly ever filled this in and I'm still trying to figure out how this might be useful to anyone. But filling it in doesn't seem to hurt either.

Titanium SDK Version

This is an important field. As features are added to the Titanium API, as things change or are deprecated, the API will change. Depending on these changes, your apps may or may not need rewrites and recompiles.

Deployment Targets

This tells Titanium what devices you will run your app on, and is important so it can generate device-specific code. Options include:

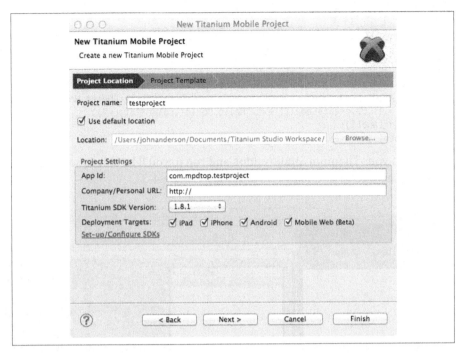

Figure 4-2. Mobile options on the Titanium Mobile Project screen

iPad

Indicates that you want your app to run on an iPad.

iPhone

Indicates that you want your app to run on an iPhone. If you select both iPhone and iPad, an iOS-universal app will be created.

Android

Indicates that you want your app to run on an Android device. I have successfully run the same *.apk* file on an Android Phone running Android 2.2, a Galaxy Tab running 2.3, and a Honeycomb Tablet running 3.0.

Mobile Web

Indicates that you want to run your project via a mobile web browser. This is a new feature of Titanium Studio and in Beta. It's interesting to play around with, but at the time of this writing it's not ready for prime time.

Writing the App

In homage to all the past "Hello World" code samples, I'll show you how you can get your first Titanium project up and running in just four lines of code that will run on iOS and Android. If you take the following code:

```
win1 = Ti.UI.createWindow({backgroundColor:"white",title:"Hello World"});
label1 = Ti.UI.createLabel({text:"Hello World",color:"black"})
win1.add(label1);
win1.open();
```

paste it into your Titanium Studio editor, and run it, you'll be able to see that it creates and runs a native iOS and native Android app (Figure 4-3).

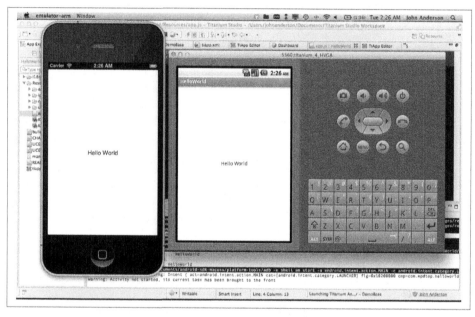

Figure 4-3. How our first app looks in iPhone and Android

This shows you how easy it can be to get an app running on iOS and Android without having to deal with learning Objective C and Java. The example is pretty straight forward, but let's go through it line by line.

This line simply creates a native window and assigns it to the JavaScript variable win1:

```
win1 = Ti.UI.createWindow({backgroundColor:"white",title:"Hello World"});
```

This line simply creates a native label and assigns it to the JavaScript variable label1:

```
label1 = Ti.UI.createLabel({text:"Hello World",color:"black"})
```

We now add the label to the window with the `.add` method:

```
win1.add(label1)
```

And finally we open the window so the UI is visible:

```
win1.open()
```

Not bad! It's fairly exciting as a developer to be able to accomplish something that's pretty significant (an app running on iOS and Android with four lines of code) with not much effort. However, a Hello World app is just the beginning, so let's move onto the next step. Next we'll look at how to create a slightly more sophisticated app using tabs and two separate windows.

Now we're ready to throw some more JavaScript at Titanium, using Titanium's library, and see what Titanium does with it. Our Hello World app will look like Figure 4-4.

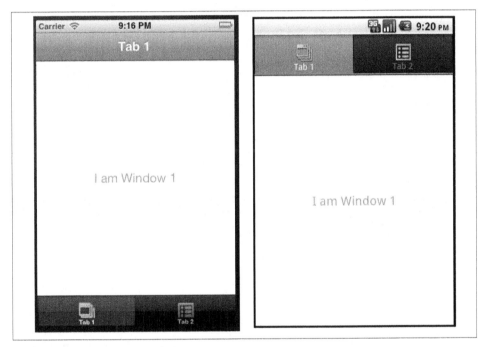

Figure 4-4. How our second app looks in iPhone and Android

```
// this sets the background color of the master UIView
// (when there are no windows/tab groups on it)
Titanium.UI.setBackgroundColor('#000');
// create tab group
var tabGroup = Titanium.UI.createTabGroup();
// create base UI tab and root window
var win1 = Titanium.UI.createWindow({
```

```
    title:'Tab 1',
    backgroundColor:'#fff'
});
var tab1 = Titanium.UI.createTab({
    icon:'KS_nav_views.png',
    title:'Tab 1',
    window:win1
});
var label1 = Titanium.UI.createLabel({
    color:'#999',
    text:'I am Window 1',
    font: {
        fontSize:20,
        fontFamily:'Helvetica Neue'
    },
    textAlign:'center',
    width:'auto'
});
win1.add(label1);
// create controls tab and root window
var win2 = Titanium.UI.createWindow({
    title:'Tab 2',
    backgroundColor:'#fff'
});
var tab2 = Titanium.UI.createTab({
    icon:'KS_nav_ui.png',
    title:'Tab 2',
    window:win2
});
var label2 = Titanium.UI.createLabel({
    color:'#999',
    text:'I am Window 2',
    font: {
        fontSize:20,
        fontFamily:'Helvetica Neue'
    },
    textAlign:'center',
    width:'auto'
});
win2.add(label2);
//  add tabs
tabGroup.addTab(tab1);
tabGroup.addTab(tab2);
// open tab group
tabGroup.open();
```

Let's go through this program section by section and see what's going on:

```
Titanium.UI.setBackgroundColor('#000');
```

This line simply sets the background color of the app's "root" view. You won't be able to see this if you have a Window or Tab Group that is opened on top of this view, and you are almost certainly going to be opening something like that in your app. It's still good to be aware that this element is present.

Two tabs get created and populated the same way, so we'll just look at one of them:

```
// create tab group
var tabGroup = Titanium.UI.createTabGroup();
```

This line creates an instance of a Native Tab Group and works equally well on iOS and Android. We use Titanium's UI object and invoke the createTabGroup method. It assigns the resulting object to the JavaScript variable tabGroup so that you can reference it later. Once initialized, the tabGroup object has all the methods and properties of the TabGroup class:

```
var win1 = Titanium.UI.createWindow({
    title:'Tab 1',
    backgroundColor:'#fff'
});
```

OK, now we're getting a little fancier. On the previous createTabGroup line, we didn't pass anything into the function call. This causes the object (in this case, the tabGroup) to be created using all the default parameters. That's not bad, but probably not something you'll do very much. Chances are you're going to want to customize it to some extent.

In this createWindow call we're passing in some parameters...or so it seems—gotcha! We're actually passing in just one parameter. This is a pretty important concept to understand so let's spend a minute or two on it. Check the parentheses and curly braces in the call, and you'll see that we're passing just one parameter to createWindow, but it contains two items—title and backgroundColor—within curly braces. The braces hold a JSON structure.

JSON (pronounced "JaSON") is a great little format that is going to make your life a lot easier in JavaScript (and is used by umpteen other systems too). It allows you to represent small or quite complex data structures and pass them around as a single object. A JSON object can be as simple as:

```
{hello:"world"}
```

Note that it's more complex than a JavaScript string, although it contains a string. We won't go into all the details of JSON right now. It's just important to realize that when you call just about any Titanium function, you pass in a single parameter that is a JSON object, which in turn contains other objects and values.

Back to our code. Our JSON object contains two parameters, title and background Color, to create a window object that's the specified title and background color. It will be assigned to the variable called win1 so that you will be able to reference it later on in the app:

```
var tab1 = Titanium.UI.createTab({
    icon:'KS_nav_views.png',
```

```
        title:'Tab 1',
        window:win1
    });
```

This command creates one of the two tabs in our tab group. The first thing to notice is how similar the `createTab` command is to the `createWindow` command. It also takes a JSON structure as the single parameter. Another thing to notice is that of the three JSON items, one is the object reference we created with the `createWindow` command (`window:win1`). The other two parameters are simply strings.

The icon parameter indicates where to find the image for the tab icon. This is a good time to point out that references like this are relative to the Resources directory in your project. Since no other path is provided in the filename, the image is assumed to be in the "root" of the Resources directory. Sometimes it makes sense to create additional folders within the Resources folder to organize your files.

If you would like to do something like this, and have an *images* folder for your images, the icon parameter needs to reflect the subdirectory, such as *images/ KS_nav_views.png* to indicate you have added an *images* directory. It's very much like referencing images in a web page using a relative path:

```
var label1 = Titanium.UI.createLabel({
    color:'#999',
    text:'I am Window 1',
    font:{
        fontSize:20,
        fontFamily:'Helvetica Neue'
    },
    textAlign:'center',
    width:'auto'
});
win1.add(label1);
```

Here we have yet another familiar "create" command, this one returning a label. As you can see, this one looks similar to the other two, with a little more information passed in. It's good to notice here that sometimes, as with the font attribute here, there will be another JSON document within the overall input parameter passed to `createLabel`. That's the power of JSON: it allows you to nest objects within objects within objects. You can represent a very complex or "rich" object with many attributes and subobjects.

It's no wonder that many public APIs, such as Google's and Yahoo's search APIs, allow the return of data in a JSON format. It also has the benefit of being totally cross platform, like XML, but in a much lighter-weight package. This is actually a key reason that JSON works well with Titanium, and enables it to work well on iOS, Android, and BlackBerry.

JSON makes good on the promise of XML: a cross-platform way to represent complex data in a compact and easy-to-consume way. XML was definitely cross platform, but not necessarily easy to consume. JSON is all that: cross platform, easy to consume, and compact for quick transfer, which makes it great for mobile.

The last thing we're going to do in this code fragment is add the label to the existing window. This is done with the statement:

```
win1.add(label1)
```

It calls the `add` method of the `win1` object and passes in the `label1` object to indicate what is to be added to the window. This is another pattern you'll get used to as you build up complex displays with nested objects: call a method on the parent or containing window and pass in the child object. Now you should start to get a feel for creating objects, assigning objects to JavaScript variables, and then using that variable in other calls to manipulate those objects.

The code sample continues with nearly identical commands to create the second window with a label, create another tab with that window, and then add a label to the second window. After that is some more assembly of the UI:

```
tabGroup.addTab(tab1);
tabGroup.addTab(tab2);
```

These two commands are relatively simple, and we see the `tabGroup` object again. Here we simply add the two tabs that we created with the `addTab` method. This is a good time to point out that many Titanium objects, such as views, support an `add` method that allows you to add new objects. The `tabGroup` object and the `NavigationGroup` are two exceptions that have different syntax. Now that we have the two tabs added, there is just one more thing to do to make our app actually do something that we can see:

```
tabGroup.open();
```

With a simple `open` method call, we're able to finally see our app. This command opens up the Tab Group and makes it visible with the two tabs. Once it's visible, you can tap on the tabs to reveal the appropriate windows. Since we know there is a label on each window, we can see that the correct window is indeed opening up when we click the tab.

On iOS, the Title Bar is automatically changed as you tap each tab. When the active window is changed, iOS reads the title of the window and puts that in the Title Bar automatically. This is a specific iOS feature, and you have the iOS view controller to thank for that. When the view controller sees that a new window is loaded up, it reads the title from that window and puts it into the title bar of the Tab Group. View

Controllers are a fundamental part of iOS, but it's one of those things that Titanium takes care of for you, so you don't have to know every detail about it right away.

Congratulations! You've created your first Titanium App, run it in a simulator or two, and walked through the code to see exactly how it works. We've seen how it's fairly easy to create and manipulate Titanium objects in the context of JavaScript, and we've seen the role that JSON plays in your Titanium apps.

The Files in Your First Project

OK, now that we've got our first app up and running, let's take a look at some of the files that are created in your project. The first thing to make note of is how your "app" is constructed in JavaScript and which of the basic files are created by default when you start your first project. Go into Titanium Studio and select New Project to bring up a dialog box that has some selections to indicate what type of project you're going to make.

For this example I've selected iPad, iPhone, and Android. Once your project is created, you'll see some new folders and files. Let's go through the important ones. All the files that have been created are listed here:

```
build folder
CHANGELOG.txt
LICENSE
LICENSE.txt
manifest
README
Resources
tiapp.xml
```

and you don't really need to pay attention to most of them right now. The important ones are:

```
build folder
Resources folder
tiapp.xml
```

The tiapp.xml File

This is an XML file that holds the configuration information for your app. Let's take a look at it now:

```
<?xml version="1.0" encoding="UTF-8"?>
<ti:app xmlns:ti="http://ti.appcelerator.org">
    <deployment-targets>
        <target device="mobileweb">false</target>
        <target device="iphone">true</target>
        <target device="ipad">true</target>
        <target device="android">true</target>
        <target device="blackberry">false</target>
    </deployment-targets>
```

```xml
<sdk-version>1.8.1</sdk-version>
<id>com.mpdtop.myfirst</id>
<name>myfirst</name>
<version>1.0</version>
<publisher>johnanderson</publisher>
<url>http://</url>
<description>not specified</description>
<copyright>2012 by johnanderson</copyright>
<icon>appicon.png</icon>
<persistent-wifi>false</persistent-wifi>
<prerendered-icon>false</prerendered-icon>
<statusbar-style>default</statusbar-style>
<statusbar-hidden>false</statusbar-hidden>
<fullscreen>false</fullscreen>
<navbar-hidden>false</navbar-hidden>
<analytics>true</analytics>
<guid>917b6e5a-25ba-41b8-8e2b-d9c5d1cb5928</guid>
<iphone>
    <orientations device="iphone">
        <orientation>Ti.UI.PORTRAIT</orientation>
    </orientations>
    <orientations device="ipad">
        <orientation>Ti.UI.PORTRAIT</orientation>
        <orientation>Ti.UI.UPSIDE_PORTRAIT</orientation>
        <orientation>Ti.UI.LANDSCAPE_LEFT</orientation>
        <orientation>Ti.UI.LANDSCAPE_RIGHT</orientation>
    </orientations>
</iphone>
<android xmlns:android="http://schemas.android.com/apk/res/android"/>
<modules/>
</ti:app>
```

You can use Titanium Studio to edit this file directly, but you won't have access to all the parameters and properties for your project. That means that the *app.xml* file contains information that is not exposed by Titanium's editor, such as enabling or disabling analytics, some of the device orientations, etc. To modify these parameters, you'll need to edit the file directly using a text editor. When you create a default project for iPhone and iPad, the "supported orientations" are set to landscape only for iPhone, and all orientations for iPad, for some reason. If you want your iPhone app to be able to support multiple orientations, you'll need to manually set that. Since the options are already there for iPad, you'll just need to copy and paste them into the iPhone section. For example, the <iphone> section of the *tiapp.xml* file looks like this by default, if you selected both iPad and iPhone when you created your project:

```xml
<iphone>
    <orientations device="iphone">
        <orientation>Ti.UI.PORTRAIT</orientation>
    </orientations>
    <orientations device="ipad">
        <orientation>Ti.UI.PORTRAIT</orientation>
```

```
            <orientation>Ti.UI.UPSIDE_PORTRAIT</orientation>
            <orientation>Ti.UI.LANDSCAPE_LEFT</orientation>
            <orientation>Ti.UI.LANDSCAPE_RIGHT</orientation>
        </orientations>
    </iphone>
```

As you can see, only landscape is indicated for iPhone, but if you want to support multiple orientations for iPhone, you can simply copy the necessary parameters from the iPad section to the iPhone section, resulting in this:

```
<iphone>
    <orientations device="iphone">
        <orientation>Ti.UI.PORTRAIT</orientation>
        <orientation>Ti.UI.UPSIDE_PORTRAIT</orientation>
        <orientation>Ti.UI.LANDSCAPE_LEFT</orientation>
        <orientation>Ti.UI.LANDSCAPE_RIGHT</orientation>
    </orientations>
    <orientations device="ipad">
        <orientation>Ti.UI.PORTRAIT</orientation>
        <orientation>Ti.UI.UPSIDE_PORTRAIT</orientation>
        <orientation>Ti.UI.LANDSCAPE_LEFT</orientation>
        <orientation>Ti.UI.LANDSCAPE_RIGHT</orientation>
    </orientations>
</iphone>
```

If you decide to implement modules, you'll need to modify the module section and put in a line for each module that you want to include. A complete *tiapp.xml* follows, with the information added to include the `tibar` barcode scanner module:

```
<?xml version="1.0" encoding="UTF-8"?>
<ti:app xmlns:ti="http://ti.appcelerator.org">
    <sdk-version>1.8.1</sdk-version>
    <deployment-targets>
        <target device="mobileweb">false</target>
        <target device="iphone">true</target>
        <target device="ipad">true</target>
        <target device="android">true</target>
        <target device="blackberry">false</target>
    </deployment-targets>
    <id>com.mpdtop.tirunner</id>
    <name>TiR</name>
    <version>1.5</version>
    <publisher>mcowner</publisher>
    <url>http://</url>
    <description>not specified</description>
    <copyright>2011 by mcowner</copyright>
    <icon>appicon.png</icon>
    <persistent-wifi>false</persistent-wifi>
    <prerendered-icon>false</prerendered-icon>
    <statusbar-style>default</statusbar-style>
    <statusbar-hidden>false</statusbar-hidden>
    <fullscreen>false</fullscreen>
```

```
        <navbar-hidden>false</navbar-hidden>
        <analytics>true</analytics>
        <guid>87a80c29-8ebb-41b1-95d5-2104d0245d15</guid>
        <iphone>
            <orientations device="iphone">
                <orientation>Ti.UI.PORTRAIT</orientation>
                <orientation>Ti.UI.UPSIDE_PORTRAIT</orientation>
                <orientation>Ti.UI.LANDSCAPE_LEFT</orientation>
                <orientation>Ti.UI.LANDSCAPE_RIGHT</orientation>
            </orientations>
            <orientations device="ipad">
                <orientation>Ti.UI.PORTRAIT</orientation>
                <orientation>Ti.UI.UPSIDE_PORTRAIT</orientation>
                <orientation>Ti.UI.LANDSCAPE_LEFT</orientation>
                <orientation>Ti.UI.LANDSCAPE_RIGHT</orientation>
            </orientations>
        </iphone>
        <android xmlns:android="http://schemas.android.com/apk/res/android"/>
        <modules>
            <module version="0.4.2">tibar</module>
        </modules>
    </ti:app>
```

Build Folder

The build folder is a folder that holds the generated projects that Titanium produces. When you run your project, Titanium creates a native project that is compiled by the native SDK. The files are located in the *build/iphone* and *build/android* directories for iOS and Android platforms, respectively. Sometimes during your development you'll want to do a "clean build," meaning that everything is built from scratch. On iOS and Android platforms, you don't necessarily have to recompile the entire project every time you want to run it.

Android used to require a full build for each and every change you made in JavaScript —"painful" doesn't adequately express how it felt working in that environment. Recently Appcelerator released a "fastdev" version for Android that gets around this. Instead of doing a full rebuild, you can simply make changes in your *app.js* or other *.js* file and your app in the Android simulator will reflect those changes. If you make changes to the *app.js* file, you'll need to exit out the of app and restart it in the simulator. If you make it in a different *.js* file, all you'll need to do is back up a few screens and go back into whatever screen would use the *.js* file that you changed. If you change the *.js* for a login page, you'll just need to exit out and go back into that login screen, and you'll see the updated screen without having to restart the whole project.

The easiest way to force a full rebuild is simply to delete the project that was generated. This will prevent Titanium from doing any kind of incremental additions, and it will have no choice but to regenerate the project.

Running Titanium Apps in the iOS simulator is easy to work with. When you make a change you're able to restart the project and run it in the iOS simulator in a few seconds. This is mainly because all the files don't need to be rebuilt all the time. This is due to features in iOS, not Titanium, but Titanium benefits greatly from this.

Even though it's good to be able to take advantage of precompiled classes to speed up development, sometimes you just need to start from scratch and rebuild everything. If you make a change in the *tiapp.xml* file, Titanium Studio is supposed to pick up on this and rebuild from scratch, but that doesn't always happen. The easiest way to ensure a full rebuild is to delete the code. Titanium has no choice but to rebuild it all.

Titanium is a great tool and makes incredible things happen. It is still a work in progress, though. Many times I'll be working on a project and putting in some simple code that I know should work. After a few attempts during which it doesn't cooperate, I'll do a full rebuild and 9 out of 10 times that fixes the issues. So, if you find yourself banging your head against the wall with an issue that doesn't seem to be going anywhere, try a full rebuild before you get too frustrated.

OK, back to the files generated by your first Titanium Project.

The place you'll be spending most of your time is in the *Resources* folder. This contains all the resources that are related to your project. It's also considered the "root" directory for accessing images from your app. Figure 4-5 shows a default resources directory.

Name		Date Mod
▶ 📁 android		Feb 4, 201
📄 app.js		Feb 4, 201
▶ 📁 iphone		Feb 3, 201
📄 KS_nav_ui.png		Feb 4, 201
📄 KS_nav_views.png		Feb 4, 201

Figure 4-5. File structure of a Titanium Project when you select New Mobile Project

When you first create a project, the *Resources* folder is pretty sparse. There's the *app.js* file (which is where your app starts from), two images, an *iphone* directory, and an *android* directory. There are some resources that apply only to iOS or Android, so these folders hold them. For instance, if you look in the *android* folders, you'll see an *images* folder with subfolders to hold splash screens for different screen densities. Similarly, in the *iphone* directory you'll see the app icon as well as several splash screens: one for iOS non-retina display, one for iOS retina display, and two for iPad (one in landscape and one for portrait). Resources that will be used on both iOS and Android will go directly in the *Resources* folder and images that are used on a specific platform will go in one of the platform-specific folders.

Events

Well, we've certainly got an app up and running, but what does it do? It displays a nice tab-based UI that contains two windows with a label. Although it looks nice (like any app on the platform you built it for) it doesn't really do much. It would be nice if it could actually show a little interaction, like a button that would show a message when pressed. Sounds good, let's do it.

We're going to get a glimpse now into Titanium Events. Events in Titanium are very similar to events in just about any event-driven programming language. In fact, my first introduction to events was when I was learning Visual Basic back in the day. I made a form, dropped a button on it, and ran it. I clicked it, and nada; nothing happened at all. After thumbing around in the manual (no Internet back then) I found out that I needed to hook a function to the "click" event. I did that, and my event-driven program (no apps yet either) was coming to life.

 Events are at the core of Titanium, as they are in many event-driven languages and systems. When invoking an event listener, Titanium almost always passes in an event object as a JSON document that gives you information about the event, what object fired it, etc.

We're going to do the same thing here. This is to show you how to attach a function call to an event, such as a button click. First thing we need to do is to add some code for the function to be called, add the button, and then hook up the button to the function call. We'll add the code to our Hello World sample right before the Tab Group open call:

```
button = Ti.UI.createButton({width:150,height:40,title:"Click Me"})
win1.add(button)
button.addEventListener('click',function(){
  alert("click me")
});
```

The first two lines should be easy to figure out, because they are yet another "create" method plus a familiar add. The other lines attach a function to the click event of the button we just added to win1. This is as basic as it gets. It's adding an inline, anonymous function to the click event. Instead of "click," you can specify any event that the button object fires. Since the button is based on a view, there are more events that you'd expect, but you probably won't use much more than the click event.

A more thorough discussion of events comes later in the book. Here I just want to let you know how events figure into the Hello World example and the rest of Titanium. The behavior of the button click is shown in Figures 4-6 and 4-7.

Figure 4-6. Basic event

Custom Events

Now that we've seen some basic events, we can look at creating our own events. Custom events are just like a built-in event on the listener side. You set up a listener as you would for any other event. The difference is that you also need to fire the event yourself, whereas built-in events are fired automatically.

The point of having a custom event is when you want to broadcast some information to listeners that may have subscribed to this event. It is a bit like calling a subroutine, except you don't need to know anything about the routine being called, other than the parameters passed into the routine. When you fire a custom event you also pass in the event information as a parameter to the function listening for the event.

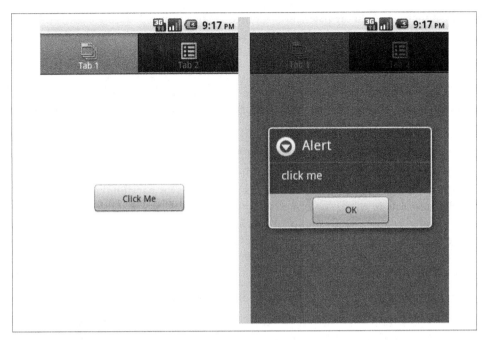

Figure 4-7. Basic event on Android

The event information that you send when you fire an event should be enough to allow the subscriber to know what's going on, but you don't want to overload it with too much information. Generally it's a good idea to pass the source of the event, so the subscriber can know what object fired the event. Once you have a handle on the event that fired the event, you can generally find out what you need.

One example of a custom event might be on an object that is handling data from a data source of some kind, which has one or more Table Views that are displaying that data. How do you know when the Table View should be updated? Well, the simple answer is that you need to update the Table View when the data source changes. Let's assume for a minute that there might be more than one table that is showing data from this data source. Also, the data source might not know how many tables are showing this data.

In this example, a custom event is a simple and elegant way to handle this. The way to handle this would be to have each table that is displaying information from the data source listen for a custom event, such as infochanged. This will allow all the Table Views listening for this event to know the data has changed and refresh themselves. This makes it easy on the data source as that object doesn't have to know how many other objects are utilizing its data.

Custom event handlers are a great way to handle scenarios such as this. They allow you to create events that will be broadcast to any objects that happen to be listening. It doesn't matter if there are actually listeners or not, you can still broadcast the event. Another way to handle that situation would be to check to see if there are any listeners, and only fire the event if there is actually anything listening on that event.

When you decide that you want to use a custom event, you have to decide what object is going to fire the event. In a scenario like a button click, it's pretty obvious that the button is going to fire the event, and that's the object that listeners will listen on, with something like:

```
button1.addEventListener('click',someRoutine);
```

The Table View situation I described at the beginning of this section is a little more obscure. We might have a data layer that is responsible for handling updates to a file. We also have one or more Table Views that want to show data from that file and want to be updated when the information in the file is updated. In this situation we're going to use the Ti.App object to fire these datachanged events. Listeners will then listen to the Ti.App object as well. Let's see how this all works.

If we're going to be firing an event through the Ti.App object, that's where the listeners need to be attached, with some code that listens for the event and the function that will run when the event is fired:

```
Ti.App.addEventListener('datachanged',function(evt){
    alert("the datachanged event has fired");
})
```

We have added a listener with an inline function that will run when the datachanged custom event has fired. The inline function will receive whatever data (if any) the event sends in the evt variable that is passed into the function. This is usually a JSON variable, which can represent several items of data in a compact format. It's a good convention to pass just one parameter in the form of a JSON document so that, as with other built-in events, there is just one parameter sent in on the event handler.

In our example, we now have a listener that is ready to receive an event. How do we fire that event? It's as simple as setting up the listener:

```
Ti.App.fireEvent('datachanged',{msg:"Something has changed"})
```

This single line of code sends the datachanged message to whatever listeners might be set up. That's it—it really is that simple. Now that we've seen the bare minimum for listening and firing custom events, let's see how this shapes up into a slightly more filled out example.

Let's accomplish something like the scenario I mentioned earlier, where we have a data source that is driving some Table Views and we want to keep those Table Views up to date with correct data. To keep track of when the data changes, we'll have a function whose job it is to write data out to a file. This will give us a place to fire the custom event through the Ti.App object. This function will then fire the custom datachanged event:

```
app = {};

app.writeToFile = function(filedata) {
    file = Titanium.Filesystem.getFile(Ti.Filesystem.applicationDataDirectory,
                                       "filetowatch.txt");
    if (!file.exists) {
        file.createFile();
    }
    file.write(filedata);
    Ti.App.fireEvent('datachanged',{newdata:filedata});
};
Ti.App.addEventListener('datachanged',
    function(evt){
        Ti.API.info("datachanged event " + JSON.stringify(evt));
    });
app.writeToFile('someddata');
```

This example defines a function called app.writeToFile that handles writing out the data to the file that we're watching, and is also responsible for firing a custom event when it is called. We then add a listener on that event that can do whatever updates are necessary when the event fires. The data that comes into the event is:

```
{"newdata":"someddata","type":"datachanged"}
```

This is the "newdata" JSON property that we sent in on the datachanged event. Titanium also adds the "type" JSON property, which is simply the name of the custom event. If you start using many custom events, this property will let you always know what event fired each notification. This can be handy if you have the same listener setup on multiple custom events.

Custom events are a nice way to do intra-app communication. It's an easy way to send information to anyone who has subscribed, or set up listeners to receive events without having to know ahead of time what those listeners are.

CHAPTER 5

Becoming a Capable Control Freak

Controls are the way mobile users do things with their devices, such as pressing buttons, choosing items from option lists, and navigating among tabs. One of Titanium's great advantages in comparison with some other environments that produce native apps is that Titanium uses native controls. When you ask Titanium for a button, the button that an iPhone user gets is the same button that a native app would use, and so on. This is a win-win-win situation, for the following reasons:

- Users running your app see and interact with native controls in the ways they are accustomed to. So on iOS, a slider looks like the same native slider users see in other apps, whereas Android users see an "Android" slider. This makes users more comfortable using the app, and ensures that the control supports all the features they expect.

- Using native controls saves you the trouble of rebuilding them in HTML5/CSS/JavaScript. HTML5/CSS is a powerful combination and gives you incredible control over the UI, and it's possible to create user controls in HTML5/CSS. But it's also a lot of work, whereas Titanium lets you create a native control with a single line of code.

- Native controls perform better and require less device resources to render and interact with. They are compiled components, so they run much more efficiently than anything you can create in HTML. Remember that anything in HTML has to run through a web browser, chromeless or not, and this is a very "heavy" layer. Native controls don't have to pass through those layers.

Now that we know the advantages of using native controls, let's see some of them in action. This is also a great, concrete way to understand the impact of using native controls in Titanium. Seeing examples like this could very well be the "aha" moment when you get a better feel for the value of using Titanium. Later I'll show how to customize the controls so they offer the convenient interactions your app needs to be slick.

Basic UI Controls

Even though Titanium works on BlackBerry, we'll focus in this chapter on iOS and Android because they hold, together, 95% of the market share of smartphones these days. Figure 5-1 shows what some common controls look like on the iPhone and an Android phone.

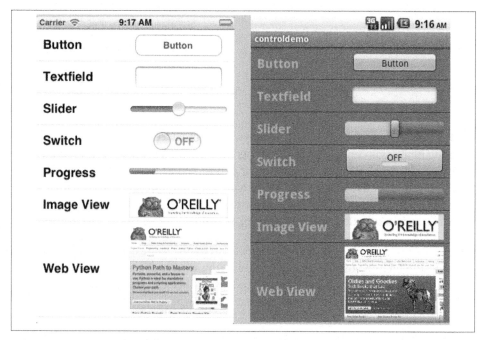

Figure 5-1. Basic UI controls are rendered as 100% native controls

Button
> The top item in Figure 5-1 is a standard button control. You can control the size and the position of the button using standard position parameters, such as left, top, right, and bottom.

Textfield
> Next we have a text field. This control, of course, allows the user to enter text. Based on the platform, it allows you to take advantage of platform-specific features, such as making the font smaller as the user enters more text. You can also specify a minimum size to keep the font readable.

Slider
> A slider is a great control allowing users to quickly select a range of values.

Switch

A switch allows a user to express a Boolean condition: on or off, 1 or 0.

Progress

Progress bars keep the user informed of time to completion during a longer than normal operation, such as downloading a file. It's useful when there is no other visual indication of what's going on, or how much longer an operation is going to take.

Image View

An image view is a handy way to display images, either stored locally or on the Internet. If you specify a URL, the Image View control will attempt to load the image at that URL. You can optionally specify a "loading" image that should be stored locally in the app. This allows you to show a custom image in case the downloaded image takes a while to download. This control can also be used to display local images.

Web View

A web view is great to display web images or simply display HTML content. Sometimes it's handy to use HTML data in your app. For instance, suppose you are writing an app that displays lots or tabular information. Formatting the data using HTML would be a great way to off-load that part of the app to web developers who are well-versed in HTML. The web files could then be handed off to the developer of the app, who integrates them into the app. When a button is pressed or the desired action happens, the appropriate HTML file could be displayed in a web view. The only caveat about this approach is that it's easy to fall into the trap of trying to put too much of the app into a web view.

Table View

Another control that isn't as obvious but is demonstrated by this app is a Table View. The other UI examples are all loaded into the table view to make an easy presentation that scrolls. A table view is a fundamental part of many apps on all common platforms. The simple yet elegant scrolling list that Apple designed and implemented so well has been copied on every mobile platform.

TableViewRow

The TableViewRow is a very useful item. When I first started working with them, I thought they were a nice way to display data in rows, but not incredibly flexible. There are a few attributes you can set to show a left image, right image, caption, and a hasChild indicator. This will cause an indicator to be displayed on the right of the row to show there is more content, like a chevron arrow in iOS.

Tablets? No Problem

It's no secret that tablets are taking the world by storm. Apple's passion for a great user experience put this category back on the map. Anyone getting involved with mobile development has to ask themselves, "Will my apps run across tablets as well as mobile devices?"

As they say, a picture is worth a thousand words, so I'll just save myself some typing and let you look at screenshots of the same app from Figure 5-1 running on iPad and Galaxy Tab (2.2.1) (see Figure 5-2).

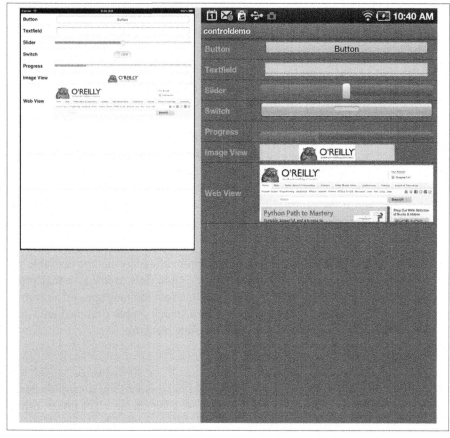

Figure 5-2. Basic UI controls as native controls on various tablets

As you can see, the aspect ratio for the Android tablets is much "taller" than that of the iPad. I think this reflects Apple's ability to know what's best for the user and to build it even if it costs more. In the end, users appreciate the better user experience, and will pay for it. Since Android tablets and phones use more "off-the-shelf" components, the resolutions and aspect ratios might not be optimal for a great user experience.

Window-Based UI Controls

You can make some very useful apps with basic controls, especially if you're developing a business app whose purpose might be to hit a backend data source and simply display some data. The UI controls we've seen so far can be placed just about anywhere, including in TableViewRows.

There are, however, some really neat controls lurking under the surface on iOS and Android. iOS continues to break new ground in terms of innovative user experiences. Android, in its turn, is good at copying what Apple comes up with.

Picker Control

The picker control (Figure 5-3) is best known for its debut as a date picker in iPhones. It was an easy-to-use, even entertaining way to pick dates with a single finger. It was innovative, clever, and just plain fun.

This is a good example of having the exact same JavaScript code render a useful control on both platforms, making the most of each platform it runs on. iOS users will be able to enjoy the deep, rich experience that they have been used to. Android users will be able to, well, select something. The important thing to remember is that the same JavaScript code will run on both platforms, taking advantage of the unique qualities of each. This is a perfect example of cross platform apps that don't take a "lowest common denominator" approach:

```
Ti.UI.backgroundColor = 'white';
var win = Ti.UI.createWindow({
  exitOnClose: true,
  layout: 'vertical'
});

var picker = Ti.UI.createPicker({
  top:50
});

var data = [];
data[0]=Ti.UI.createPickerRow({title:'Bananas'});
data[1]=Ti.UI.createPickerRow({title:'Strawberries'});
data[2]=Ti.UI.createPickerRow({title:'Mangos'});
data[3]=Ti.UI.createPickerRow({title:'Grapes'});
```

```
picker.add(data);
picker.selectionIndicator = true;

win.add(picker);
win.open();

// must be after picker has been displayed
picker.setSelectedRow(0, 2, false); // select Mangos
```

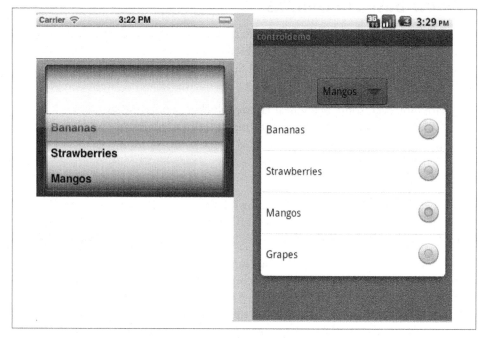

Figure 5-3. Cross-platform picker control

The picker control is a handy way to give the user an easy way to make a single selection from a list, with a minimum of muss and fuss. It's also clear that the picker control was designed to work the way a mobile user would most likely be using their phones. It's easy to flick the picker list up and down with your thumb and tap your selection.

It doesn't take long to understand the power of the momentum principle pioneered by Apple. To move a few items down the list, just give it a gentle nudge. To get to the end of the list fast, give it a powerful flick and the list will fly down, making noise like a Geiger counter along the way.

Option Control

An option control (Figure 5-4) is another Window-based UI element because it has modal operation—that is, it requires user confirmation before turning control back to the app, so it can't be embedded in a page or a TableViewRow. In iOS, it has a "slide up" effect, coming up from the bottom of the current window and presenting you with one or more options and usually a Cancel button.

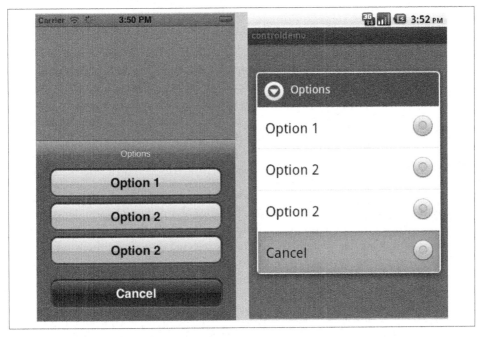

Figure 5-4. Cross-platform option control

The control makes it easy for a mobile user to select the desired option by simply tapping a selection, or tapping the Cancel button to say "none of the above." The Cancel button also gives the user an easy way out if he accidentally invokes the option:

```
var dialog = Titanium.UI.createOptionDialog({
    title: 'Options',
    options: ['Option 1','Option 2','Option 2','Cancel'],
    cancel:3
});

var win = Ti.UI.createWindow({backgroundColor:"white"})
win.open();
dialog.show();
```

The option picker in principle is fairly similar to the select list, except that the Option Dialog has a limited number of items that it can display. In the slide up display on iOS, you can see that there's only room for a couple more options. The picker control, on the other hand, can handle many more items since you can scroll through the list, whereas an Option Dialog is limited to the amount of space on the slide up panel.

Creating Your Own Composite Objects

We've seen how to create standard Titanium objects (windows, buttons, switches, etc.) and how to add things to a standard control (a TableViewRow, in this case) to create a customized look. But often the basic controls in Titanium can't accomplish the job all by themselves. By combining basic controls in an object you define, you can create your own composite controls and toss them around in your program conveniently.

Let's think of what a simple color picker might look like. It might contain an area showing the currently selected color plus three sliders that the user can slide to control the R, G, and B values of the color. The selected color will be shown in a view whose background color we'll set based on the slider values. As for the three sliders, we need additional controls that a plain slider doesn't include. There should be a label saying Red, Green, or Blue on each slider so the user knows which slider controls which value. It would also be nice to show the currently selected value (from 0 to 255) on a label by the slider.

Your first instinct might be simply to create all the necessary components and place them appropriately in the window that displays the color picker. Three sliders could be placed on the window at the proper coordinates, along with the labels for the name of each slider and the slider value that is currently selected directly on the window. This would work, but it wouldn't be a great way to do it. If you wanted to insert another slider in between two existing ones, or move the existing ones around, you'd plunge into needless grunt work.

In short, custom controls are a great way to encapsulate multiple UI elements and custom event handlers into a single cohesive unit that can be used with a few lines throughout your app.

The Customized Slider Object

The robust solution to combining controls is to create your own little control factory in JavaScript. This factory is a JavaScript function that builds up the necessary components into a JavaScript object that it returns to the calling process. Although some people who have seen a lot of old, poorly structured JavaScript assume that it's old-fashioned and inferior to "serious" programming languages, JavaScript is actually well endowed with the means to create and manipulate objects in a modern style.

So in JavaScript, you can define a function that creates any type of Titanium objects, sets defaults or values passed in by a caller, and then returns the completed objects. This allows us to quickly make composite controls with any degree of specialization we want. Each control can have its own properties and methods. So for instance, if you want to reflect the slider's value as an integer from 0 to 255, you can write a method to do it and every slider will behave the way you want.

Creating a control factory will have several benefits:

- It will be easier to create the controls your app needs. You'll just issue one line of code, instead of instantiating all the lower level controls each and every time.
- If you need to change the look and feel of your control, or its behavior, you'll just need to change it in one place instead of every place that you created that control.
- If you are building up your own function library for your own use or for the use of other developers, they now have easy access to your design across projects.

In this section we'll create a custom slider that includes a representation of the slider's value as an integer from 0 to 255. As laid out in the previous section, the three base items we'll use to build this control are a label on the left, a slider on the right, and a view to hold them. Our factory creates three objects—label, slider, and view—and adds the label and slider to the view, which is the object returned to the caller.

Just so you have an idea of what we're shooting for, Figure 5-5 gives a sneak peek of the slider control as it will look in the finished product. I've added a red border around each Titanium base object so you can see how they all fit together.

Figure 5-5. A custom slider control

We'll adopt the Titanium convention we saw in the previous chapter, where each constructor accepts a single object. We'll expect the caller to pass a JSON structure. This way, we can define as many parameters for our object as we like, and the caller can specify as few or as many as it wants. Defaults will fill in the rest. Our factory will be called like this:

```
ctlLabel = makeSlider();
```

ctlLabel now points to an instance of our customer slider, just as win1 pointed to a window we created in the previous chapter.

Out actual function looks like this:

```
makeSlider = function(config) {
    view = Ti.UI.createView(config);
    view.height = 45;
    view.borderRadius = 5;
    view.label = Ti.UI.createLabel({
        left:10,
        width:45,
```

```
            top:11,
            height:22,
            text:"000",
            color:"white",
            font:{
                fontSize:20
            }
        });
        view.add(view.label);
        slider = Ti.UI.createSlider({
            right:5,
            left:60,
            top:10,
            min:config.min,
            max:config.max
        });
        view.add(slider);
        slider.addEventListener('change',
            function(evt){
                this.parent.label.text = (this.value).toFixed(0);
                this.parent.fireEvent('customevent',
                                {
                                    src:this.parent
                                });
        });
    return view;
};
```

The first several lines should be easy to understand at this point in your reading. We create a view and set various properties, including the label, which we add to the view. We then create a slider and add it to the view.

Now we add an event listener, as introduced in the previous chapter:

```
slider.addEventListener('change',function(evt){
    this.parent.label.text = (this.value).toFixed(0)
    this.parent.fireEvent('customevent',{src:this.parent});
});
```

These lines of code add an event listener to the slider so that when the slider moves, the function registered by the listener will be called, passing in the evt variable, which is a JSON document with information about the event. The next line updates the value of the associated label to show a numeric representation of the value of the slider.

Now when the user slides the slider, generating a change event, our control will change the value of the label. Note that the keyword this can be used in an event handler, and will refer to the object that fired the event. After updating the label, a custom event is then fired called customevent to any listeners that are attached to that event. This also passes in the JSON document {src:this.parent} as the event object to those listeners.

One subtlety distinguishes the label from the slider. The label is defined as one of the view's properties (view.label), whereas the slider is a separate object. We make the label a property of the view because the view is the object returned to the caller, and we want later to find the label when an event is called. By making the label a property of the view, we can get to the label through the this object in our event handler. But we never have to get to the slider in an event handler, so it doesn't have to be a property of the this object.

 Titanium doesn't offer a very easy way to retrieve objects added to a custom object. The choices are the getChildren() function and the solution I use here, a custom property. There is no way to directly access an object within the custom object. A compromise is to place a custom attribute on any object that you create, which would allow you to directly access the object associated with that attribute. This allows you to get quick and easy access to child objects, assuming that you set a custom attribute on the parent object before or after you added the child object.

When an event fires, the event listener automatically gets an event object that has a reference to the object that fired the event. I've called this event object evt. If some manipulation needs to be done on the source object, the reference gives us access and we don't need to go hunting for the object. Similarly, custom attributes on the source object gives us easy access to child objects that a view, for instance, may contain. Once a change event fires on the slider, we know that the slider has moved due to some user interaction. We simply need to update the label on view. This is done with a single line of code:

```
this.parent.label.text = this.value.toFixed(0)
```

Knowing that this refers to the slider, we use the .parent property to find the containing view and then find the label within the view. The code will always find the label corresponding to the slider that was moved, even when multiple sliders are in the app firing events. The line then sets the value of the label with the current value of the slider, adjusted to eliminate decimal points. The min and max values for the slider are passed in when you call the factory. This allows you to specify different min and max values on each slider control that you create.

Although many Titanium objects share common properties, there are a few unique ones based on the type of control that is being used. For example, on our slider example, we use a native slider control that is created by a JavaScript line of code like this:

```
slider = Ti.UI.createSlider({
    left:10,
    right:10,
    backgroundColor:"#777",
```

```
        min:0,
        max:255,
        top:10
    });
```

In this example the min and max properties control the highest and lowest value the slider will return. This doesn't control the physical size of the control at all. It merely controls the highest and lowest value the slider will return based on the position of the slider control.

The src property of our parameter, evt, refers to the same thing as this. We use it in the last line of the event listener. This gives us an easy way to refer to the source event that fired the event that we are processing.

 Composite controls must be self-contained and not use any global variables. Always expect there to be multiple controls of the same type firing events that call the same event listener code. Take care to make sure they won't step on instances of their clones.

Now let's look at the full app that calls this control factory:

```
app = {
    win : Ti.UI.createWindow({
        backgroundColor:"#bbb",
        layout:"vertical"
    }),
    makeSlider : function(config) {
        view = Ti.UI.createView(config);
        view.height = 45;
        view.borderRadius = 5;
        view.label = Ti.UI.createLabel({
            left:10,
            width:45,
            top:11,
            height:22,
            text:"000",
            color:"white",
            font:{
                fontSize:20
            }
        });
        view.add(view.label);
        slider = Ti.UI.createSlider({
            right:5,
            left:60,
            top:10,
            min:config.min,
            max:config.max
        });
```

```
            view.add(slider);
            slider.addEventListener('change',
                function(evt){
                    this.parent.label.text = (this.value).toFixed(0);
                    this.parent.fireEvent('customevent',
                                    {
                                        src:this.parent
                                    });
                });
            return view;
        },
        init : function() {
            sliderConfig = {
                left:10,
                right:10,
                backgroundColor:"#777",
                min:0,
                max:
                255,
                top:10
            };
            slider1 = app.makeSlider(sliderConfig);
            slider1.addEventListener('customevent',
                                function(evt){
                                    //alert(evt.src);
                                });
            app.win.add(slider1);
            app.win.add(app.makeSlider(sliderConfig));
            app.win.add(app.makeSlider(sliderConfig));
            app.win.open();
        }
    };
    app.init();
```

Our little mini-app here consists of two sections, the slider factory called makeSlider and the init() function. makeSlider is simply a JavaScript function that creates our custom object.

Figure 5-6 shows the app running on iOS and Android. Notice how similar the screens are on the two systems. Except for the status bar on the Android screen, the controls on the two screens look nearly identical. However, each uses the native basic controls of its platform.

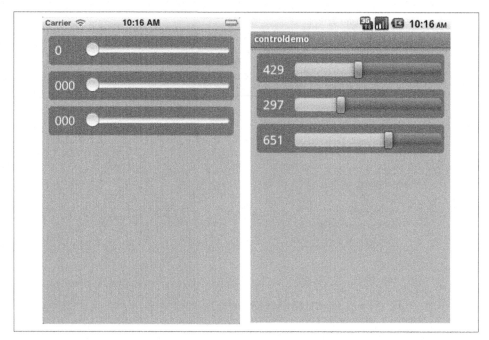

Figure 5-6. Cross-platform custom slider

As apps become more complex and require more composite controls, defining them through a factory can be a real time saver. You can make customized controls that work across platforms without having to write a custom module (described later in the book). Because all the base objects being used to make the composite control work across platforms, so will any composite controls made from those base controls. This approach on commonly used objects can make you and your team more productive. It provides a central place to store the objects, and if a change is needed, it can be updated easily in one place instead of many.

Custom Attributes on Controls

As we've seen in the previous section, it's advantageous to limit your event listeners to the bare minimum. With event propagation, you can add event listeners at a high level that will get multiple events. The most common kind of high-level event handler is on a TableView. A TableView has multiple rows, and it doesn't make sense to add an event handler on each row.

This is most definitely a good thing, but a single function called on those events will be getting events from multiple objects. The trick then becomes knowing which object the event actually came from. In a TableView, each row could potentially have objects that fire events, which could propagate up the object hierarchy. So how does that one function sort out where the event came from and what it should do?

Some built-in attributes help your function figure out what to do. When you place event listeners on a `TableView`, the event object has an index attribute designating which `TableViewRow` the event came from. But, what if you have multiple objects on each `TableViewRow` that could potentially fire the event?

Custom attributes are a great way to add custom information to your objects. JSON, which as we've seen is used throughout Titanium, lets you tack your own bits of information onto objects. When an event fires, you can look inside the "source" object in the event object to see the custom attributes that have been placed on it.

 Think of custom attributes as cheat sheets that can easily be stuck in the "pocket" of a TableViewRow, slider, or any object. This makes small pieces of information easily accessible and handy, especially in event handlers.

Custom attributes can be useful in a few different ways. One example might be an app that does a search on an ISBN database. Perhaps you'd enter an author name into a web service and get back data for that author. You'd want to display a table with the books by that author, with the ability to tap on a row to show more information. A way to handle this would be to use custom attributes as you're building up the table rows. You could attach a few attributes to contain the extra information that you would want to display upon tapping the table row.

Custom attributes on objects can also make your application much snappier. Instead of making a web service call every time a row is tapped, call the web service once to get all data related to an event. The extra data can be put on each row so that when the row is tapped, the existing data can be displayed, instead of making the user wait for another web service call to complete.

You have the choice of passing several separate custom attributes or passing a single custom attribute that is a JSON object containing multiple parameters. Which is better? Sometimes it boils down to a matter of what you're more comfortable working with. If you have a small number of attributes, passing multiple single-purpose attributes are fine. Once you start passing more complex data, JSON documents are a good way to make it easy to access the information, as well as allowing it to be self-documenting to an extent.

Actually placing the custom attributes is incredibly easy. Since we're working in Java-Script, we're able to extend our standard objects with custom attributes by simply setting the values, such as the following:

```
obj = Ti.UI.createTableViewRow({});

bookdata = {};
bookdata.authorName = "Anderson, John";
```

```
bookdata.ISBN = "99999";
bookdata.bookTitle = "Up and Running";

obj.bookData = bookdata;
```

The JSON document `bookdata` would likely have come as part of a web service call, but we're just doing it inline now to make the example a bit easier to follow.

Retrieving this data is as easy as setting it. When you are in the event handler, you'd be able to retrieve the previous data with something like `evt.source.bookdata.ISBN` and have easy access to the data. This is a very handy technique and makes the app easier and quicker to write. Here's a sample of how to make a web service call to retrieve some data and tack a JSON document onto each row with extra data:

```
app = {
};

app.mainWindow = Ti.UI.createWindow({
    backgroundColor:"white"
});
app.mainWindow.open(); var xhr = Ti.Network.createHTTPClient();
xhr.onload = function(){
    retdata = JSON.parse(this.responseText);
    rowData= [
    ]; for (i=0;i < retdata.rows.length ; i++) {
        row = Ti.UI.createTableViewRow({
            title:"row " + i
        });
        row.extraData = retdata.rows[i];
        rowData.push(row);
    }
    table = Ti.UI.createTableView();
    table.setData(retdata);
    app.mainWindow.add(table);
};
xhr.onerror = app.errorCallBack;
xhr.open("GET",
        "http://somewebservicecall",
        false);
xhr.send();
```

The example assumes that the web service call returns a JSON document. When the callback is invoked, it parses the document and loops through it. As it builds each table row, it sets a custom attribute called `extraData` and assigns the JSON document that pertains to that row. The neat thing about this is that when a row triggers an event, the row will be passed into the event handler. It will then be easy to see the `extraData` attribute on the row, and get whatever relevant information might be needed.

An important thing to make note of here is that there isn't any kind of database involved in this example. Even though there are some rich data stores being used, it's all attached to UI components and very easy to access. It's a good example of putting the data in a convenient place so that it's available when you need it.

That convenient place is on the UI component that generates the event; in this example, it's the `TableViewRow` object. By setting a custom attribute on it, that data is available in the event handler via the `evt.source` object. When the event is fired the event object has a reference to the event source, which includes the custom attributes we put on it.

As you build more and more Titanium apps, you'll find that custom attributes on objects, especially JSON documents that can hold complex data, will be a real time saver and help simplify your apps.

More Uses for Custom Controls

Another handy use of the factory technique might be to build your own `Naviga` `tionGroup` object. Because the object model for a `TabGroup` is pretty much like the `NavigationGroup`, it might be nice to define a custom object that makes them more similar. This would be fairly easy to do with an approach similar to the custom slider.

As a quick refresh, the `TabGroup` is an object that you can issue `open()` directly and to which you add tabs. The `NavigationGroup` is an object that needs to be added to a base window. When that base window is opened, the `NavigationGroup` would open additional windows that need to be brought into view.

Using a custom factory, we can make our own `NavigationGroup` object that acts more like a `TabGroup`. The function will take one parameter that becomes the root window for the `NavigationGroup` group, the one that is visible. The code looks like this:

```
createNavigationGroup(config) {

    rootObj = Ti.UI.createWindow();❶
    rootObj.navGroup =
        Ti.UI.createNavigationGroup({window:config.rootWindow});❷
    rootObj.openWindow = function(config){ this.navGroup.open(config) };❸
    rootObj.add(rootObj.navGroup);❹
    return rootObj;

}
```

❶ Create the base window that will contain the `NavigationGroup`.

❷ Create the `NavigationGroup` itself with the window passed in as its base window.

❸ Add a custom method to the `NavigationGroup` to be used to open a new window inside the `NavigationGroup`.

❹ Add the `NavigationGroup` to the base window, after which you can return it as a new object.

This allows you to create a complete `NavigationGroup` object with a call like this:

```
rootwin = Ti.UI.createWindow();
navgroup = createNavigationGroup({window:rootwin});
navgroup.open();
```

Creating custom controls keeps you in control (pun intended) and allows you to set up the parameters to reflect the way that you work best. For example, let's think about a `NavigationGroup` some more. When you want a navigation group, all you're really worried about is something to control your windows and open them up in the right UI.

When you make a `NavigationGroup`, you don't want to worry about creating a base window that no one will see, but that still needs to be there. You don't necessarily want to worry about creating all the ancillary objects and build them up into a single object that can be used like you want to. Ideally, you'd want a one-line command like this:

```
win1 = Ti.UI.createWindow(title:"Root Window");
navGroup = TiCL.UI.createNavigationGroup({window:win1})
navGroup.openGroup();
```

This is easy to remember and lets you concentrate on what you want to happen in the app. You just want to get a `NavigationGroup` up and running with your own window inside of it. And this is where encapsulating this functionality in a factory really shines.

In fact, when I was looking through the iOS source code one time, I even saw some comments in the code that Appcelerator wanted to go this route with the `Naviga tionGroup`, making it more like the `TabGroup`. It's much more natural to think about creating a base window, be it a `TabGroup` or a `NavigationGroup`, and then open up that object and add objects to it.

The great thing about custom objects is that we don't have to wait for Appcelerator to do it, or live with their implementation when they do. We can create our own custom objects, giving them behavior and attributes to suit the way we work.

The Main Event

We touched on events earlier in the Hello World example, but let's take a look at them in a little more detail now.

Events are the way an object (base object or custom object) tells the app that something has happened. When you want to monitor for a specific event, you add a listener to it. Below, we see how to add an event listener to the Hello World example to show a message when a button is tapped:

```
button.addEventListener('click',function(){
alert("click me");
});
```

What we did was to add an unnamed "inline" function via the addEventListener method call. Since we're using standard JavaScript here, we can pass in either the name of a function or a function itself. To keep things really simple, we passed in a function itself that simply pops up a message box.

One thing missing is a parameter on the function call. As we saw earlier in the chapter, when Titanium fires events, it includes an event object that is passed to the function. The handler is defined to accept only one parameter, but like most things in Titanium, it's a JSON object, so it can contain all the information you will ever need. Well, it will contain a lot of information about the event that has been fired.

Let's change our Hello World event a little bit to include the event parameter so we can see what's going on:

```
button.addEventListener('click',function(evt){
Ti.API.info(evt)
});
```

We've made two changes:

1. We added the event parameter to the function call.

2. We logged information from the event parameter that gets passed in.

So what happens now is that when the button gets tapped, it logs the following information to the Titanium console:

```
{
    globalPoint =       {
        x = 172;
        y = 247;
    };
    source = "[object TiUIButton]";
    type = click;
    x = 87;
    y = "19.5";
}
```

As we discuss events, keep in mind that different events add different types of information to the event object. The best way to see what you have to work with is to log it to the console. What you see before you is a nice little summary of useful information about a click event, formatted as a JSON document. There are basically five properties on this event:

globalPoint
    The absolute screen position where the tap was made.

source
    The object that generated the event. The braces in [object *className*] represent another, nested JSON object.

type

    The name of the event, which correlates directly to the event name you used in `addEventListener`. In this example, it's `click`.

x and y

    The position on the screen that was clicked relative to the object that generated the event. So if the user clicks in the upper-left corner, these will be close to 0.

The best way to get to know what events pass in what data on the event parameter is to just play around with events and objects. Issuing `Ti.API.info(evt)` or `Ti.API.in fo(JSON.stringify(evt))` is the best way to see the data coming in. Sometimes it will be a lot and sometimes it will be minimal.

Event Propagation

You can't talk about event handling very long before you get into event propagation (or event bubbling). You're not exactly sure what that is? Well, it's kind of neat. Let's talk about it with a good example, and one that apps use quite a bit: a table view.

Event propagation is the traveling of events up to the parents of the objects on which the events fired. Event propagation allows a high-level object to get notified of events fired on its child objects. This can help keep the number of installed listeners to a minimum, which helps memory usage and performance.

Let's say you have a `TableView` containing five rows, and each row has two buttons on it. There are actually a few places that you can add event handlers. You could assign an event listener on each button in the `TableView`, on each row, and on the table itself.

When an event fires on one button and is not handled by that button, it is then fired on the parent `TableViewRow`. If the `TableViewRow` does not catch it either, the event is fired on the `TableView`. In short, the event travels up to each parent in the hierarchy until it reaches the window object. This allows us to place an event handler on the `TableView` instead of each button in the `TableViewRow`.

The whole point of event propagation is that it allows you to monitor many events by placing a few event listeners. Keep in mind that every call to `addEventListener` consumes some memory and increases the overhead of the app on the CPU. In our table containing five rows with two buttons each, you might be tempted to add an event listener to both buttons on all five rows. That would be bad because you would have 10 listeners waiting for the buttons to fire. Even if your event listeners are calling the same function, you still have 10 times the overhead necessary.

A better solution is to add event listeners to each row. This way you're cutting down your event listeners in half, which is good. But, there would still be one event listener for each row. In some situation where you could end up with many rows, you'd have many event listeners, which isn't great. So we might as well economize even more and place the event listener on the whole table. Let's see how we'd do this in code:

```
tableview = Ti.UI.createTableView();
rowData = [];
for (i=0; i < 5; i++) {
  row = Ti.UI.createTableViewRow();
  btn1 = Ti.UI.createButton({left:10,height:30,width:75,title:"Button1"});
  btn2 = Ti.UI.createButton({right:10,height:30,width:75,title:"Button2"});
  row.add(btn1);
  row.add(btn2);
  rowData.push(row);
}
tableview.setData(rowData);

tableview.addEventListener('click',function(evt){
  Ti.API.info(evt);
})

win = Ti.UI.createWindow();
win.add(tableview);
win.open();
```

The main thing to take note of here is that we have a single event listener on the table, instead of every individual element that might fire an event. Here is the event information that comes through when we click on the row:

```
{
    detail = 0;
    globalPoint =      {
        x = 232;
        y = 124;
    };
    index = 2;
    row = "[object TiUITableViewRow]";
    rowData = "[object TiUITableViewRow]";
    searchMode = 0;
    section = "[object TiUITableViewSection]";
    source = "[object TiUITableViewRow]";
    type = click;
    x = 232;
    y = 16;
}
```

Make note of the source property on the event object. This shows that the event was fired from the TableViewRow and not the button. Here is the event information when one of the buttons is tapped; see how the source property has changed:

```
{
    detail = 0;
    globalPoint =      {
        x = 66;
```

```
        y = 52;
    };
    index = 0;
    row = "[object TiUITableViewRow]";
    rowData = "[object TiUITableViewRow]";
    searchMode = 0;
    section = "[object TiUITableViewSection]";
    source = "[object TiUIButton]";
    type = click;
    x = 56;
    y = "25.5";
}
```

There are many events that will be firing in any mobile app. The key to a well performing app is to keep the number of event listeners as low as possible. This is achieved by putting event listeners at a point where a single listener can handle events for multiple objects.

CHAPTER 6

Titanium Objects

Now that we've seen some of what Titanium can do, let's take a look at some of what's running things behind the scenes. iOS and Android platforms are very object-oriented, with everything in the app represented as one object or another.

Many objects share common properties and methods. Titanium has a number of base objects (the View being the most frequently inherited from) that all the other objects are based on. This allows you to know what kind of properties, methods, etc. are available on an object that is based on a view. For instance, a view has width and height properties. Since a button is based on a view, then a button also has width and height properties. At a UI level, most objects have these common properties and make it easier to know what you can do with a given object.

App Object

The App object is a good one to start with because it gives you access to things that happen at the "App" level. It represents the currently running app, and serves as a namespace that is available to any process running in any window in the app. This means that an event handler anywhere in the app can always access the App object. Depending on how you set up your namespace in your app, this may or may not be true of JavaScript objects that you create.

The App object contains interfaces to some very useful functions, such as the ability to store app-related data easily, capture events when the app goes into the background and comes back into the foreground, fire local notifications, and run "services" in the background. Let's look at some of these features in more detail.

Storing Data in the App Object

Items stored in this object will persist across application sessions, meaning that if the app is shut down and started up again, this information will be present when the app is restarted.

The App object is good for storing things such as application preferences, though it's not an interface to the Settings panel that you sometimes use in an iOS app to set some app preferences. It's an object that allows you to store anything that you can serialize into a string.

The API interface that stores data in the App object resides in the App.Properties namespace. The data types this supports are Boolean, Double, Int, List (Array), and String. These different data types allow you to store values from JavaScript in their native format. The format to store and retrieve data is simply a "set" or "get" followed by the data type, such as:

```
arr_chapters = ['one','two','three'];
App.Properties.setBool("isrunning",false);
App.Properties.setDouble("bignumber",34340934034);
App.Properties.setInt("pageNumber",22);
App.Properties.setList("chapters",arr_chapters);
App.Properties.setString("amGreeting","Good Morning...");
```

These are some simple uses of the App.Properties object to store some data in your app. Just remember that this object is best for bite-sized pieces of data that need to be accessible from any object in your app.

App.Properties is a great place to store small amounts of data in their native types. It's good for simple app settings or preferences. As you start putting more data in this object, ask yourself whether it needs to be here, or if it can go into a file or a database. The bottom line is that if you're wondering whether you should store something in the App.Properties object, you probably shouldn't.

The setString method lets you store any kind of string data, which means you can store JSON objects. The App.Properties object can store a string representation of a JSON object, but can't store the JSON object directly. Store an object created through JSON.stringify and use JSON.parse to unpack the string after you read it. Again, remember that when your data starts getting more than bite-sized it might be better to just write it out to a file.

Pause and Resume Events

Probably one of the most useful aspects of the App object is some of the events that it gives you access to. Since iOS 4.0, apps were able to enter a background mode, which allowed them to keep their state and have some limited functionality. When you wanted to run it again, you could select it from your background apps and it would wake up and be at the same point you left it. A few App events allow you to know when your app has entered the background mode (become inactive) or entered the foreground mode (become active again):

pause

> This fires when the app goes into the background for any reason, such as the user getting a phone call, hitting the home button to get back to the main screen, etc.

resume

> This will fire when the app returns to the foreground, except when it is returning to the foreground from a pause by an incoming phone call.

resumed

> This will fire when the app returns to the foreground from a pause by an incoming phone call.

Although it is possible to see when your app goes into background, and comes into the foreground as the app is paused and resumed, there are limits to what can happen in the background. The main things that an app can do in the background is play music and get location updates.

Adding event handlers to the App object is the same as registering a listener for the click event on a button, or any other event, as seen here:

```
Ti.App.addEventListener('pause',function(evt){
  Ti.API.info("app went into the background");
});
Ti.App.addEventListener('resume',function(evt){
  Ti.API.info("app went into the foreground");
});
```

These two statements can register small functions that will log when the app goes into the background and back into the foreground. Catching the pause event can help your app know when it's not being actively used and act accordingly. There is usually a small amount of time during which the app can do anything before iOS puts it to sleep. Once this happens, only some kind of notification or the resume event will cause it to wake up and be able to do anything again.

As useful as running background tasks might be, be aware there are restrictions over what can be done, such as receiving location updates or playing music. When you make use of the resume function, anything that can be done in an app can run at this time. This is due to the fact that after the resume event, your app is running in the foreground and can do whatever it needs to.

Background Services

Another rather neat part of Titanium is its ability to run a background service. This is similar to the pause event that you can put some code in, but gives you a bit more flexibility. The pause event runs for a fairly short amount of time before the app goes to sleep. There is some time to log some data or do some fairly quick, simple tasks.

The background service is more robust in that it gives you more time for your process to run, usually about 10 minutes before iOS prevents it from running. This is a good amount of time to do some more complex processing, although they are still subject to Apple's restrictions on what can and cannot be done while the app is in background mode.

Setting up a background service in Titanium is quite easy. You basically just need a file for the code that you want to run in the background, *bg.js* for example. In your main app code, you then register this file to run when the app goes into background mode:

```
var service = Ti.App.iOS.registerBackgroundService({
    url:'bg.js'
});
```

And then in the *bg.js* file you simply put the code that you want to run. The big gotcha to be aware of is that the background service runs in its own context outside of your main app. This means that even global variables that you set up in your app won't be accessible from the service.

To be able to pass information between the contexts of your main app and any background services that you might be running you will need to write the information to the device's filesystem or use `Ti.App.Properties`. `Ti.App.Properties` is an integral part of Titanium and therefore IS accessible by your background service.

Local Notifications

Titanium's App object exposes two types of notifications in iOS and Android: push notifications and local notifications. Both appear the same to the app and are delivered with the same information. The difference lies in how they are originated. Push notifications are originated outside of the app and outside of the phone, whereas local notifications are originated on the phone itself. We'll be looking only at local notifications in this book.

Local notifications are originated by your app at some point when the app is running. They can be set to fire on a regular schedule (hourly, daily, weekly) or just fire once at a predetermined time. The nice thing about local notifications is that they will fire even if the app isn't running.

A classic example of using local notifications builds on one of the App events that we learned about earlier in the previous section, the pause event. Since the pause event fires when the app goes into the background, we have a few precious seconds in which to do something before the app goes to sleep. In this example, we'll set up a local notification to fire 5 seconds after the app goes into the background.

We'll be using a background service for this example so you can see a little more of a real-world example of how background services work. The background service will be registered exactly like we did in our previous example, and the *bg.js* will be enhanced to schedule a local notification. When the app goes into the background, the *bg.js* code will kick in automatically and schedule the local notification.

A good thing to point out here is that the app isn't doing anything with the local notification other than asking iOS to run it at the given point in time. In our example, we're scheduling it for a few seconds after the app goes into the background. In reality, it could be hours, days, or weeks in the future. This way, your app just needs to ask the mobile OS to run the notification and then it's up to the OS to show it at the appropriate time. *bg.js* now looks like this:

```
var date = new Date();
var notification = Ti.App.iOS.scheduleLocalNotification({
    alertBody:"App was put into background ",
    alertAction:"Re-Launch!",
    userInfo:{"hello":"world"},
    sound:"pop.caf",
    date:new Date(new Date().getTime() + 3000) // 3 seconds after backgrounding
});
```

When this code runs in a background file, such as the *bg.js* we registered earlier in the app as a background service, the code will run when the app goes into background mode. It contains a single `scheduleLocalNotification` method that causes the local notification to be displayed 3 seconds after the app goes into the background.

The local notification call takes just a few parameters:

alertBody
> The main text of the alert. The name of the app will show up as the title of the alert.

alertAction
> The text that is to show up on the button that the user will press to launch the app, if she chooses to do so. The launching of the app will also call whatever event listeners are present for a notification event.

userInfo
> A nice little "back pocket" to put some information that you want the push notification to carry along with it. If you have listeners in your app for location notifications, those listeners will have access to this information. Push notifications take on a much more useful purpose if you make use of this information. By using this property, your app can automatically respond to a push notification to do something such as bring the user to the screen he needs to be on. The more useful a push notification is, the more your users will enjoy responding to them instead of just hitting Close.

sound
> Simply an optional sound that the notification can play when it appears on the device.

date
> The date and time that the local notification should show up on the device.

Window and View Objects

A window object is basically the UI canvas or page where you place UI elements for the user to view. Any app you build needs to open up at least one window, or you won't see anything past the splash screen. You'll offer a better user experience by creating a window, adding objects to it, and then opening it. If you open the window and then add UI elements, your users could see the individual controls being added in the course of a few hundred milliseconds.

The reason this happens is that when the window is open, it automatically updates the UI with any window changes. Since you make changes to the window with individual JavaScript commands, these changes are reflected in the visible UI as they happen. When the window hasn't been opened yet, the objects are added while the UI isn't visible. When you then open the window, the controls have already been added and the UI is presented with the controls already there. It's just a good practice so that the user experience is a bit smoother.

Windows and views are the two fundamental building blocks that the UI layer of apps are built on. Windows are usually the topmost object in the UI layer "food chain" (Figure 6-1). The exception to this is where there is an object as the base object that can contain other windows, which we'll go over later in the chapter.

An important distinction between windows and views is that you can add views to a window, but you can't add another window as a child of a window. However, you can add more views to a view.

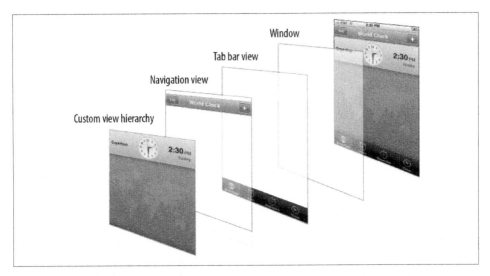

Figure 6-1. Window and View layers in an app

This makes views very handy for holding a few objects that need to be grouped together. Once you put your objects into a view, you can move the view around and the child objects will move around as well. Consider the following example:

```
app = {
};
app.init = function() {
    app.mainWindow = Ti.UI.createWindow({
        backgroundColor:"white"
    });
    app.mainWindow.open();
    view1 = Ti.UI.createView({
        top:0,
        borderColor:"red",
        layout:"vertical",
        height:250,
        backgroundColor:"#666"
    });
    view1.add(Ti.UI.createButton({
        title:"Button 1",
        top:20,
        height:50,
        left:40,
        right:40
    }));
    view1.add(Ti.UI.createButton({
        title:"Button 2",
        top:20,
        height:50,
        left:40,
```

```
        right:40
    }));
    view1.add(Ti.UI.createButton({
        title:"Button 3",
        top:20,
        height:50,
        left:40,
        right:40
    }));
    app.mainWindow.add(view1);
};
app.init();
```

As you can see, the three buttons are inside a view. The buttons are added to the view and the view is then added to mainWindow (Figure 6-2). The other way to do this would be to add the buttons directly to mainWindow, but this would require you to change the position of each button separately. By placing them inside a view, you can later change the view's position and all its children will move along with it.

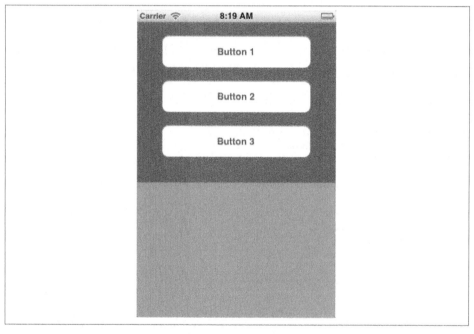

Figure 6-2. Using a View to control groups of controls

In addition to making layout chores a bit easier, adding several components to a view as we're doing here can also make events easier to consolidate. As we saw in the previous chapter, it's better to have event handlers at a higher level, rather than on individual components, such as the buttons in this case.

You can easily set an event handler on the view to track events that happen on the view, as well as the children of the view—in this case, the buttons. Sticking to one event handler allows you to process all the events by a common routine, as well as keep the event listeners down to a minimum.

Here's the same app with the event listener added on the view. Since this routine will be processing the events for the view and any child in the view, we need to know which object fired a click event, for example. That's where some custom attributes come in handy. Having a custom attribute on each object, such as key, allows you to know which object fired the event by looking at evt.source.key:

```
app = {
};
app.init = function() {
    app.mainWindow = Ti.UI.createWindow({
        backgroundColor:"white"
    }); app.mainWindow.open();
    view1 = Ti.UI.createView({
        top:0,
        borderColor:"red",
        layout:"vertical",
        height:250,
        backgroundColor:"#666",
        key:"theview"
    }); view1.add(Ti.UI.createButton({
        title:"Button 1",
        top:20,
        height:50,
        left:40,
        right:40,
        key:"btn1"
    })); view1.add(Ti.UI.createButton({
        title:"Button 2",
        top: 20,
        height:50,
        left:40,
        right:40,
        key:"btn2"
    })); view1.add(Ti.UI.createButton({
        title:"Button 3",
        top:20,
        height:50,
        left: 40,
        right:40,
        key:"btn3"
    }));
    app.mainWindow.add(view1);
    view1.addEventListener('click',
        function(evt){
            alert(evt.source.key);
        });
```

```
};
app.init();
```

Another type of view that can make your mobile life easier is a scroll view. Scroll views are basically identical to a non-scrolling view with the notable exception that their content area is scrollable. This is another reason why it's good to use views where you can, as it's very easy to go from a non-scrolling view to a scrolling view.

As you can see, views can give you tremendous power both in the UI aspects of your app and in consolidating event handlers for the objects in those views. When used correctly, views can make your programming life much easier.

Window and View Layout

Now that we've seen how views can be helpful, let's look at one of the more helpful parameters on a `Window` or `View` object, the layout property. This property controls how the child objects are laid out inside of a view or window.

Layout

The layout property is deceptively simple. It takes one of three values:

absolute

> The absolute mode of laying out child objects is very similar to the same term in CSS positioning. In other words, the top and left position you give are exactly where it is positioned, no ifs, ands, or buts. Titanium doesn't try to do anything other than place the item exactly where you tell it to be placed.

horizontal

> The horizontal layout mode is a little different. It starts laying out content at the left most edge and then adds components, working towards the right edge as long as there is enough horizontal space. When there is no more space, it "wraps" and continues laying out content underneath the original component.

vertical

> Vertical layout is similar in operation as the horizontal, except that it lays things out vertically, top to bottom.

Let's take a look at examples of each of these. For the examples, we'll use the following code to see the effect of the layout parameter on child objects. An important thing to notice is that we didn't specify any layout parameter on the window object, so it will default to absolute. This simply means that the objects will be placed at the absolute position specified by the top and left parameters for each object.

When you use absolute layout and don't specify any top or left parameters to position the object, Titanium will center the object in the middle of the screen, horizontally and vertically, based on the width and height. If you don't specify a width and height, they will default to the entire screen. So if you're running this app without being familiar with Titanium, it would be very easy to think that only one button was added. In reality, all three buttons are indeed being added. But since we specified no left and top positions, they all default to the same position and are actually being stacked one on top of the other.

If you use absolute layout, either by default or by choice, Titanium will place objects at an absolute position based on the top and left parameters of the object. If you don't specify anything, Titanium will center the objects, which could result in objects layered on top of each other.

A good way of adding the button objects to the window would be to populate the top and left parameters with meaningful values. The code here creates the buttons from our previous example, but with some good values that allow the buttons to be placed so they can all be visible when the app starts up:

```
app = {
    win:Ti.UI.createWindow({
        backgroundColor:"#bbb"
    }),
    btn1 : Ti.UI.createButton({
        top:50,
        width:90,
        height:40,
        title:"button 1"
    }),
    btn2 : Ti.UI.createButton({
        top:100,
        width:90,
        height:40,
        title:"button 2"
    }),
    btn3 : Ti.UI.createButton({
        top:150,
        width:90,
        height:40,
        title:"button 3"
    }),
    init : function() {
        app.win.add(app.btn1); app.win.add(app.btn2); app.win.add(app.btn3);
        app.win.open();
    }
};
    app.init();
```

This will give you some output like in Figure 6-3.

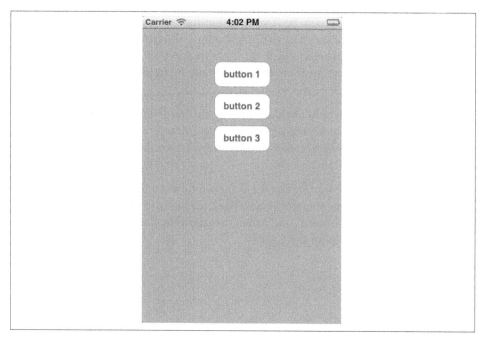

Figure 6-3. Adding controls with the default layout of absolute

It's also worth noting that if you only specify "left" or "top," Titanium will still center the object for the property that you didn't supply. In our example, we are only specifying the top parameter, to get the buttons to not be stacked on top of one another. Since we didn't specify the left parameter, Titanium still centers that dimension, which works nicely for our purpose.

Most of the times, the vertical layout will be more suitable than absolute as a starting point. To look at how vertical layout affects how the buttons are added to the window, we'll make one small change in the `createWindow` line to have it use a vertical layout:

```
win:Ti.UI.createWindow({layout:"vertical",backgroundColor:"#bbb"}),
```

With just this small change, the window's initial view is much different (Figure 6-4).

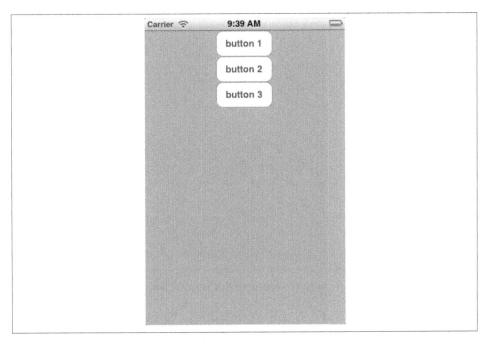

Figure 6-4. Adding controls with a layout of vertical

Now we see that the window has added all three child buttons, placing the first at the top of the window and simply starting the next button flush against the last one added. Since we haven't specified an explicit left and top position, Titanium is simply keeping track of the height of the last element and starting the top of the next element directly under that. So if we changed the height of the middle element to 100, the last element will adjust itself accordingly, as you can see in Figure 6-5.

Now if we change the window layout mode to horizontal, with the following change, we'll see how the buttons are now laid out starting flush on the left, inserting them horizontally flush next to each other (Figure 6-6):

```
win:Ti.UI.createWindow({layout:"horizontal",backgroundColor:"#bbb"}),
```

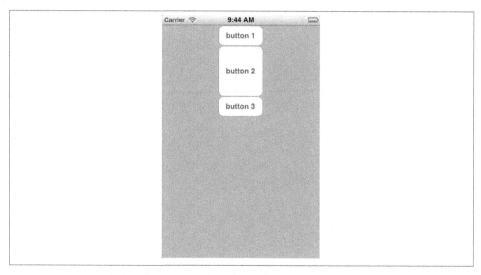

Figure 6-5. Controls flow from top to bottom with vertical layout

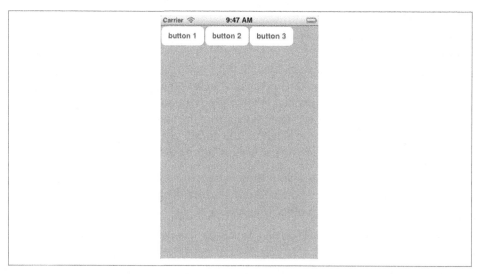

Figure 6-6. Adding controls to a window with horizontal layout

As in vertical layout, if we change the widths of the child objects, the next object will still be placed flush against the previous one. Titanium dynamically calculates where the next object should start based on where the last object ended.

If there is not enough room horizontally to fit in the new control, Titanium will place the next objects on the next "line" under the first object placed. Here we see how this works, by adding more buttons of different widths:

```
app = {
    win:Ti.UI.createWindow({
        layout:"horizontal",
        backgroundColor:"#bbb"
    }),
    btn1 : Ti.UI.createButton({
        width:70,
        height:40,
        title:"button 1"
    }),
    btn2 : Ti.UI.createButton({
        width:170,
        height:40,
        title:"button 2"
    }),
    btn3 : Ti.UI.createButton({
        width:120,
        height:40,
        title:"button 3"
    }),
    btn4 : Ti.UI.createButton({
        width:70,
        height:40,
        title:"button 4"
    }),
    btn5 : Ti.UI.createButton({
        width:70,
        height:40,
        title:"button 5"
    }),
    btn6 : Ti.UI.createButton({
        width:150,
        height:40,
        title:"button 6"
    }),
    init : function() {
        app.win.add(app.btn1);
        app.win.add(app.btn2);
        app.win.add(app.btn3);
        app.win.add(app.btn4);
        app.win.add(app.btn5);
        app.win.add(app.btn6);
        app.win.open();
    }
};
app.init();
```

Figure 6-7 shows that the layout manager in Titanium stacks the child objects one after each other horizontally until it runs out of space, and then continues on the next "line" as it adds more objects. The one useful layout or option that isn't present in Titanium would be to center the content dynamically. It could behave the same as horizontal, but instead of starting on the left, it could center the content on initial layout. It would then re-center the content as items are added.

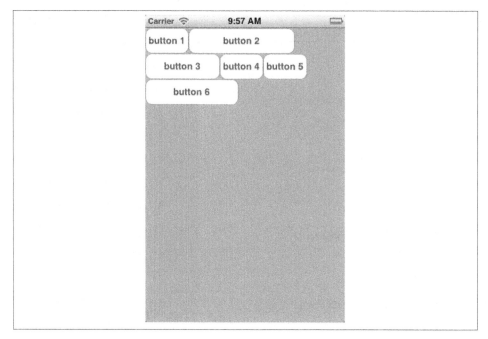

Figure 6-7. Horizontal layout with controls of various widths

View Controllers

A View controller is pretty much what it sounds like. It's an object that controls multiple windows or views. There are several standard types of UI interactions that can be built into apps. The two most common of these on iPhones is a Navigation View Controller and a Tab View Controller. Titanium calls these NavigationGroups and TabGroups, respectively.

Before we start talking about NavigationGroup, TabGroup, and SplitView controllers let's talk about View controllers at a bit higher level. It's important to know how this works "under the hood," especially with iOS.

View controllers are responsible for controlling a set of child windows. Titanium conceals this from you somewhat as a developer, but it's always good to know how it implements your requests. Because the View controller is responsible for presenting the overall display, the View controller usually handles the title bar while the window controls the area under the title bar. The View controller sets items in the title bar, such as the title and the back button title based on information in the window. The window therefore indirectly sets some of the information presented by the View controller.

When a window is active, the NavigationGroup reads information from the window object so that it knows what information to show in the title bar, back button, etc. For instance, when the NavigationGroup opens up another window, it reads the title property of the child window to set the title bar caption. Thus, view controllers take care of things such as nice transitions between windows, setting the title bar caption correctly, setting the back button title, etc. All you have to do is instantiate the type of control you want and add to it the visible views that it will show the user.

Without understanding the role of the View controller, it's easy to make the mistake of trying to do things like set the title on the title bar directly. The NavigationGroup reads the title from the window and uses that to automatically update the title bar.

With a good appreciation of what View controllers bring to the party, it's a little easier to use them. As long as all the information is set up correctly on the windows you create, View controllers make it easier to give your apps a robust user experience.

Navigation Group

A Navigation Group contains other windows. As we talked about already, the Navigation Group handles the transition between windows. Instead of doing something like win.open(), you would do something like navGroup.open(win). This allows the Navigation Group to add the window as one of its children and then make the window visible while sliding the current window out of sight.

Figure 6-8 shows the relationship between the Navigation Group and the child windows. Each of the child windows will be able to contain TableViews, WebViews, etc.—any kind of UI element that can be added to a window. After the Navigation Group opens it, the window is a child of the Navigation Group.

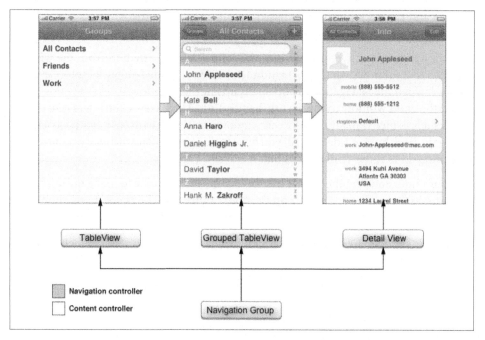

Figure 6-8. Navigation Group and child windows

The Navigation Group is available only on iOS. In Android, when you open up multiple windows, it automatically provides a Navigation Group–like experience, sans title bar. When you already have a window open in Android, and you open up another one, a slide transition reveals the new window. The hardware back button will then take you back to the previous window and destroy the one you are navigating away from.

Navigation Groups are similar to a Tab Group, but for some reason it's not quite as easy to get your head around it as the Tab Group. Here is some sample code that creates a Navigation Group:

```
var mainWindow = Ti.UI.createWindow();
var rootWindow = Ti.UI.createWindow({
    title:"First Window",
    backgroundColor:"white"
});
var navigationGroup = Ti.UI.iPhone.createNavigationGroup({
    window:rootWindow
});
mainWindow.add(navigationGroup);
mainWindow.open();
```

This produces the screen in Figure 6-9.

Figure 6-9. Navigation Group with one default window

It's important to point out that the mainWindow, however necessary, will never really be seen. Its role is to provide a full screen window to contain the Navigation Group, which in turns holds the rootWindow that *will* be seen, and which will control the caption in the title bar.

This layering gives working with a Navigation Group a little more of the DIY feel, since you have to build the overall object up with what seems like separate objects. This contrasts a little bit with the TabGroup object, in that you simply create the object, add tabs to it, and then open the TabGroup object.

There's not really much purpose in having a Navigation Group unless you're navigating between groups of windows...right? So let's add a button that takes us to other windows and look at how that works, along with the Back button. Here's the new code that we'll run to accomplish this:

```
var mainWindow = Ti.UI.createWindow();
var rootWindow = Ti.UI.createWindow({
    title:"First Window",
    backgroundColor:"#bbb"
});
var navigationGroup = Ti.UI.iPhone.createNavigationGroup({
    window:rootWindow
});
var btn1 = Ti.UI.createButton({
```

```
        title:"Open Window 1",
        top:150,
        width:200,
        height: 40
    });
    btn1.addEventListener('click',
        function(evt){
            var win2 = Ti.UI.createWindow({
                title:"Second Window",
                backgroundColor:"#bbb"
            }); navigationGroup.open(win2);
        });
    rootWindow.add(btn1);
    mainWindow.add(navigationGroup);
    mainWindow.open();
```

The new code just creates a button and an event handler for the click event. When the user clicks the button, it creates a new window and asks the Navigation Group to open it. It's very important to understand that the Navigation Group is opening the window instead of just doing a `window.open()`, which would certainly be possible to do. Because the Navigation Group opens the window, the Navigation Group can manage that window within the existing group of child windows.

So, now we've got an app with a button that opens up a new window within the current Navigation Group when the user clicks the button, and we end up with something like Figure 6-10.

There are a couple things to note here. When we create and open the Navigation Group initially, we don't give it any information for the caption in the title bar directly. By virtue of adding the first window, which does have a title, we give the Navigation Group what it needs to populate the caption in the title bar.

Similarly, when we open the second window, the Navigation Group is able to:

1. Transition the first window out by sliding it to the left.

2. Transition the second window in by sliding it to the left.

3. Animate the Navigation Group title to transition between the first and the second titles.

4. Program the back arrow to provide a means to get back to the first window, and at the same time reverse all the animations when it is pressed.

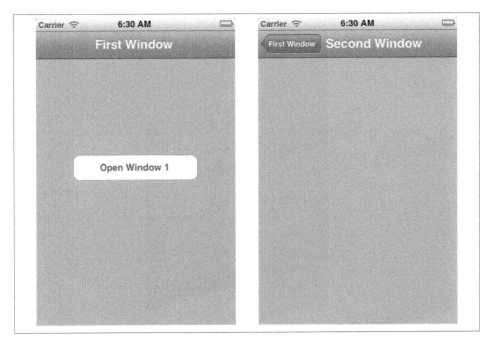

Figure 6-10. Navigation Group with one default window

I think that you can start to understand and appreciate the role that a view controller can play in managing a group of windows in your application. By simply creating windows and setting a few attributes on them, you're able to create a robust, interactive app that gives people the user experience they have come to appreciate on iOS.

On Android, creating the same situation is a bit less complicated. You basically just need to open windows as needed. Since the Android OS was developed with the assumption that the standard hardware buttons are present, the process is a little easier. Open your first window. When you need to transition to another window, simply create it and open it. The user viewing the second window can simply press the hardware back button to return to the first window.

TabGroup Object

Tab Groups are nice UI elements to break up a lot of information into some digestible pieces. Tabs are UI elements that have been around forever, and make a nice translation onto mobile devices as long as there are just a handful of tabs.

Similar to the Navigation Group, you don't open the windows directly in a Tab Group. You add windows to a tab, add the tab to the Tab Group, then open the Tab Group (Figure 6-11). Thus, windows are added to Tab Groups in a slightly different way from a Navigation Group. With a Navigation Group, the children are the windows themselves.

With a Tab Group, the children are tabs, with each child tab having a window as its child. It might sound a little confusing, but makes sense after you work with it for a few minutes.

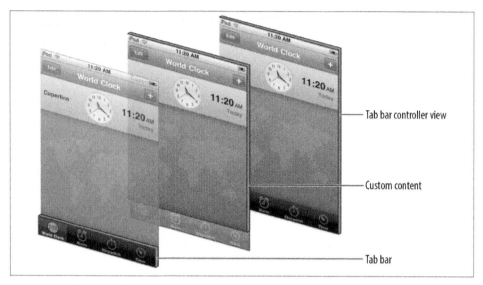

Figure 6-11. Tab Group interface

Both a Navigation Group and a Tab Group manage a set of windows and provide a certain user experience with certain UI characteristics. A Navigation Group allows you to "navigate" through a set of windows with slide transitions. A Tab Group allows you to access windows by tapping on a tab and jumping between windows in whatever order you want.

Tab controllers share the basic "controller" functionality of the NavigationGroup object, managing child windows and the transition to and from those child windows. It also shares the behavior of updating the title bar based on information from the active child window.

The basic procedure for setting up a tab view is what we saw on our first test project. Here is some code that creates a basic Tab Group with two tabs (see Figure 6-12):

```
app = {
    tg : Ti.UI.createTabGroup(),
    win1 : Ti.UI.createWindow({title:"win1",backgroundColor:"#aaa"}),
    win2 : Ti.UI.createWindow({title:"win2",backgroundColor:"#aaa"}),
    init : function() {
        app.tab1 = Ti.UI.createTab({title:"Tab 1", window:app.win1});
        app.tab2 = Ti.UI.createTab({title:"Tab 2", window:app.win2});
        app.tg.addTab(app.tab1);
        app.tg.addTab(app.tab2);
```

```
            app.tg.open();
        }
    }
app.init();
```

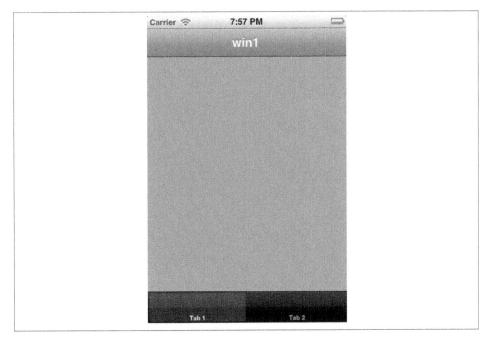

Figure 6-12. Tab Group and child tabs

This Tab Group contains two tabs, each tab containing one window. This is a very easy way to set up a screen with multiple windows on it that give the user easy access to them all via an easy-to-use interface.

Conclusion

Titanium objects hold a wealth of power ready to serve your needs. The best way to learn how to use these objects is to simply play around with them. Nothing beats getting your hands dirty, just getting some code running, and seeing what it's all about.

CHAPTER 7

Customizing Titanium

The previous chapters have given you an overview of Titanium's language, namespaces, objects, and methods, hopefully offering you plenty of neat stuff to work with. But Titanium's foundation in JavaScript also makes it easy to extend and customize. JavaScript lets you create your own prototype functions that add functionality to any class you want. For instance, you can easily create a string prototype function that adds functionality to any string object created in JavaScript, like this:

```
String.prototype.trim = function() {
    return this.replace(/^\s+|\s+$/, ''); };
```

This line of code adds a `trim` function to any JavaScript string object you create. Prototypes are a very cool feature of JavaScript and should be exploited profusely. They allow you to add functions that perhaps you've gotten used to in other languages and would like to take advantage of while working with Titanium.

You can also make "mini-factories," which are basically functions that create Titanium objects with certain properties or other traits that you'll need regularly. Creating these mini-factories will allow you to have a central point where you can make changes, and all the calls to these factories will return an object with those changes in it.

What's in a Name...Space

Titanium contains many separate objects, making them available via namespaces. In general terms, a namespace is an abstract container that provides a context for the items that it contains.

The topmost object in the Titanium namespace is just `Titanium`, or `Ti` in its shorthand equivalent. `Titanium.UI.createWindow` is exactly the same as `Ti.UI.createWindow`. You don't have to spend too much time typing out "Titanium" over and over before you appreciate being able to use "Ti" in method calls.

The namespaces under Ti organize all the method calls within the namespace logically. Every function call needs a unique name, and clashes can be avoided by putting similar calls in the same higher-level namespace. This also provides some modest documentation. So you'll know that user interface-related calls will be in Ti.UI, whereas geospacial functions will be in Ti.Geolocation.

So how does this affect customization? It's important to understand how namespaces work and how they are organized, because in this chapter, we're going to be talking about making our own functions that act similar to Titanium's built-in functions. Instead of just having a bunch of arbitrarily named functions, we're going to organize them into our own namespace, so that it's easy to find them later.

Depending on how large of a company you work for, others might want to make use of your customizations as well, so it's a good idea to make your functions easy to understand and use.

 As you move towards making Titanium your own, it's important to have some kind of strategy about how to organize things at a level higher than an individual programmer. I've seen too many times where decisions such as these are made without much departmental consensus, let alone ownership at the company level.

There's a saying that goes "If you don't know where you're going, you'll probably get there." A similar thing could be said about trying to make customizations to Titanium without some collective agreement on what should or shouldn't be in it, and how it should be organized. Without some ownership and collective agreement, all you'll end up with is a inconsistent framework addition that will probably waste more time that it will save.

Titanium Compatibility Layer (TiCL)

Out of the box, Titanium probably has about 80% true platform independence. This means that about 80% of the code that you can write will run on iOS and Android (leaving BlackBerry out of the picture for a moment) without any kind of modification at all.

The other 20% comes from the fact that Titanium just works slightly different on different platforms. For instance, if you're creating a window and adding buttons to it, you use the .add method on the window to add the created buttons. One difference between iOS and Android is that when you call .add on iOS, you can pass in an array of buttons or other objects to be added. On Android you can't; you need to call .add once for each object.

Obviously 80% is a high number, but the ultimate goal would be to have it running at 100%. There are situations where you might need to check what platform you are running on, and then do things differently based on the individual platform. After writing a few apps that I wanted to run across multiple platforms, I soon realized that I was going to be writing the same "if-iOS-elseif-Android" code to do the same thing over and over for future apps, so I decided to make my life easier by writing what I call a "compatibility layer," in a new namespace I invented named TiCL. It provides a thin interface of functions I defined that can take care of these cross-platform differences outside of the application. Instead of writing your app directly to the Titanium API, you write your app to the compatibility layer API, and thus achieve nearly 100% cross-platform compatibility. If there are differences in the API between platforms, then these are smoothed out in TiCL, and not in your app.

In addition to functions that help mitigate cross-platform issues, you might want to create some "convenience functions" for yourself. There are plenty of situations in Titanium when you want to do a certain task, such as write some data to a file, that requires a few lines of Titanium. When you're getting started, a few lines doesn't seem too bad, but after a while, you'll find you want to keep your source code as compact as possible. Convenience functions also help speed up your development, because you can insert one easy-to-remember function instead of a collection that might not be so easy to remember.

Another example of a convenience function is one that authenticates a user. This could be a relatively complex function to code from scratch, depending on the requirements of your company. It could involve some knowledge of Active Directory, setting up a web service for the mobile app to call, some server-side coding to do the lookups in Active Directory, etc. However, if someone already did all the legwork to make this work, then all you have to do is call an API such as the following:

```
TiCL.Security.authenticateUser(
    domain,userid,password,
    success_callback,fail_callback
);
```

When organizing my compatibility layer, I shamelessly copied the method names in Titanium. This is where it's important to understand namespaces. To get my namespace up and running, I simply created an empty JavaScript object and assigned some second-level objects to it. I did this because I wanted to mimic the original Titanium method names. So if I needed my own createButton method, the whole call would be TiCL.UI.createButton(). This makes it easy to know what methods to call, because they are exactly the same as the standard Ti calls.

The custom namespace is set up like this:

```
TiCL = {};
TiCL.UI = {};
```

```
TiCL.Util = {};
   ...
```

You basically need to decide what name your namespace is going to start with (in my case, TiCL) and what the second-level namespace elements will be. It's not a bad idea to mimic the Titanium namespaces as I've done. That way, if you have developers familiar with Titanium, they can just use the standard method names but insert your namespace, as I did with `TiCL.UI.createButton()`.

Create a new *.js* file for your compatibility layer or convenience functions. This will allow you to isolate all your customizations in one file, which will be easy to include in other apps through `Ti.include`. You'll then be able to call all your custom functions.

Version and Sharing Considerations

As I mentioned, when you're developing applications for a sizeable company, it makes even more sense to make your own compatibility layer or customizations. This way, you and other developers can share the routines that you've come up with. Especially at the beginning, your own TiCL will probably evolve quickly as you find more interesting things to put into it.

The challenge then becomes managing a master copy of the TiCL and making sure you are compiling the up-to-date one into your apps. It's also good to put a version number on different versions of your TiCL so that app developers can know they are using the correct version.

Here's a small example:

```
TiCL = {

   ver : 1.5.6,

   IO : {
     fileWrite : function(filename,data) {
          ...
     }
   },

   UI : {

   }
}
```

Copying and Merging

As you work more with Titanium, adding more interactivity to your apps, you'll find that interacting with existing objects is a key part of a good app. This interaction is done by reading and setting properties, calling methods, listening for events, etc. Especially as you start building functions that create composite components, you'll want to set different properties on the base components before you return them to the caller.

This is done fairly easily and succinctly when you are creating the object. You call something like this:

```
Ti.UI.createButton({top:10,left:10,width:20,height:20})
```

and you get your button with the right properties. But you'll soon find out that when you want to start interacting with the object, or set various properties in your own control "factories" that modify the object's properties, code unfortunately becomes a bit more verbose. If you create a button and want to modify four properties, you'll end up with something like this:

```
btnChangeMe.top = 50;
btnChangeMe.left = 75;
btnChangeMe.width = 200;
btnChangeMe.height = 100;
```

This quickly becomes bulky and annoying. Getting tired of it, I wrote two convenience functions called copy and merge. These allow you to modify multiple properties of an existing object with the brevity of a single configuration object, such as the one you wrote when you created the object. So the operation that previously took four lines of code can now be done in one, like this:

```
TiCL.Utils.merge(btnChangeMe,{top:50,left:75,width:200,height:100})
```

To me this just feels more natural and I don't feel like I'm wasting a bunch of keystrokes typing out an object name time and time again.

The merge function looks through the parameters that you pass in and sets a property on the object if it doesn't exist. An important feature, though, is that merge won't overwrite an existing parameter of the same type. In contrast, the copy function goes through all the properties passed in and simply overwrites them all.

In case you want to include these functions in your own compatibility layer, here they are:

```
copy : function(config1,config2) {
    var i;
    for(i in config2) {
        config1[i]=config2[i]
    }
    return config1;
},

merge : function(config1,config2) {

    var i;
    for(i in config2) {
        if ( !config1[i] ) {
```

```
                    config1[i]=config2[i]
                }
        }
        return config1;
    }
```

Further Compatibility

Another use of the compatibility layer is to create "proxy" functions for true Titanium functions that allow you to change the config parameters. For example, take these three objects:

Ti.UI.Button
> A button caption set with a title parameter.

Ti.UI.Label
> A label caption set with a text parameter.

Ti.UI.TextField
> A text value retrieved/set with a value parameter.

These three very common UI objects contain a text element as a major part of the object, but requiring three different parameter names. It becomes a little confusing sometimes which objects use which parameters to set the text element.

One way to get around this is to create your own custom objects. For instance, let's say that we wanted to create three custom objects to handle the differences in the way the text value is set and just use textValue on all three. This attribute name is fairly self explanatory and has relevance on all three of the objects.

To do this, we need to create three objects in our own namespace. We'll start with the Button object. As we get into this process, we'll see that there are all sorts of customizations that we can place on our own objects, but I'll discuss just a couple of them in this example. The code for a basic custom object that allows us to use our new text Value parameter is the following:

```
TiCL = {

  UI : {
    createButton : function(config) {
      retobj = Ti.UI.createButton(config)
      retobj.title = config.textValue;
      return retobj;
    }
  }
}
```

This is a very basic factory object for a Ti.UI.Button object. All it does is create a standard Titanium button and set its title parameter from our own textValue. All these custom functions are contained in the TiCL top-level namespace so that we can have the same function names as the Ti namespace without any conflict. This allows us to create our own custom button with a very similar syntax, seen here:

```
myButton = TiCL.UI.createButton({
    textValue:"hi there",
    top:10,
    left:10,
    width: 100,
    height:40
});
```

When this new function is called, it takes the parameters passed into it and calls the standard Titanium createButton function. This returns a standard button in the proxy function. We'll now do the same thing for the Label and TextField controls:

```
createLabel : function(config) {
    retobj = Ti.UI.createLabel(config)
    retobj.text = config.textValue;
    return retobj;
},
createTextField : function(config) {
    retobj = Ti.UI.createTextField(config)
    retobj.value = config.textValue;
    return retobj;
},
```

We can now create proxy objects that return true Titanium objects, but we can put some of our own custom code in when they are created. This allows us to come up with our own naming conventions for different aspects of object creation.

So far, we've just provided an alternate means of setting attributes at the time of object creation. If we want to add some more functionality that we can use at runtime, we need to add some of our own custom functions onto the objects.

We created a way to set the text object value with a common config parameter name of textValue. We could add functions to our base object that would make it easier to manipulate this value at runtime, in addition to creation time. So we expand our button example a bit by adding two methods, getTextValue and setTextValue:

```
createButton : function(config) {
    retobj = Ti.UI.createButton(config)
    retobj.title = config.textValue;
    retobj.getTextValue = function() {
        return this.title;
    }
    retobj.setTextValue = function(textValue) {
        this.title = textValue;
    }
    return retobj;
}
```

Now we can get the button's text value and set it to a new value at runtime. We can similarly add these functions to the TextField and Label objects with the exact same function names.

We've seen here how to create factory objects using our own custom JavaScript routines. The proxy object creates a "real" Titanium object and then manipulates it as we see fit before returning it to the caller. This allows us to add our own configuration properties and standardize on the same parameter names across objects.

We've also seen how to add our own functions to Titanium objects. In the example we went through, we created simple getter and setters. You can add more complicated functions that do more or work with existing properties, or provide additional functionality.

Finally, you can create your own unique objects that combine two or more base objects. For example, you could use the base HTTP and Ti.App.Properties objects to create your own HTTP object with some unique built-in caching that doesn't exist in the base objects. The following code snippet provides this functionality, along with an example of calling it. The goal is to add caching to the common task of loading a URL. We can potentially speed up the application by retrieving contents from a local cache instead of repeating a call over the network to remove a web page every time the user requests the same page:

```
app = {};   ❶
app.util = {   ❷

    loadUrl : function(url,method,callback,errorcallback) {   ❸

        var xhr = Ti.Network.createHTTPClient();   ❹

        xhr.onload = function() {   ❺
            Ti.App.Properties.setString(url,this.responseText)   ❻
            callback(xhr.responseText,xhr.foundInCache);   ❼
        };

        xhr.foundInCache = false;   ❽
        doc = Ti.App.Properties.getString(url,"not found")   ❾

        if (doc != "not found") {   ❿
                xhr.foundInCache = true;
                xhr.responseTxt = doc;
                xhr.onload();
            } else {
                xhr.open(method,url,false);   ⓫
                xhr.onerror = errorcallback;
                xhr.send();
        }
    },
}
```

```
success = function(result,cached) {  ⓬
  alert("got something in the custom callback cached = " + cached)
}
app.util.loadUrl("http://www.oreilly.com","GET",success,"")  ⓭
```

❶ Define the app variable, which serves as the top level namespace for the entire app.

❷ Add a second-level namespace, util, to the app namespace. This will be set to an object that contains functions. Right now, the only function in this object is loadUrl, but it could contain many functions.

❸ This is the signature for the function, which takes four parameters.

❹ Create an HTTP object for us to use to make the URL call.

❺ Set the function to be called for the onLoad event. This event will fire after the HTTP call is made and the data from the call has been received.

❻ Cache the result of a successful HTTP call. It is stored in the Ti.App.Proper ties object mainly to keep this example brief. A slightly better way to store this information in a production app could be writing to the local filesystem, with a filename based on the URL.

❼ Invoke the callback routine indicated by the callback variable passed into the function. This allows us to call a passed-in function in lieu of using the unload event built into the Titanium HTTP object.

❽ Initialize the default value of foundInCache to false. It will be set to true later if it is found.

❾ Check the cache to see whether the contents of the URL were stored from a previous call. If nothing is found, return the text not found.

❿ If there is a cached result, use it when calling the callback function that was passed in.

⓫ If the URL is not in the cache, make the HTTP call. As seen in #5, this invokes the "internal" callback routine, which in turn caches the result in Ti.App.Prop erties and calls the "external" callback that was passed in as part of the loa dUrl call.

⓬ Define the "external" callback function that is called by the loadUrl function after the internal processing is done. We pass in the result of the call and a Boolean flag to indicate whether the result was in the cache or not.

⓭ Here we call the loadUrl function to put all our hard work into action.

The preceding code is a good example of using some base Titanium objects to create another object that will make your life easier, and to provide some functionality that doesn't exist as written. This object contains a custom routine that wraps up a "base" object and makes it easier to use. There are a few parameters that you need to set when you use the HTTPClient in Titanium, and it's not always easy or desirable to try to remember them all. Using a function like this, you can invoke one line of code that has some fairly easy-to-remember parameters. This makes it easy to work with because you don't have to stop and look up the parameters every time you need to use it.

The sky (you know, that thing that holds "the cloud") is the limit when you start thinking about creating proxy objects that conform to how you like to work, or making new objects that don't exist yet. A key thing to remember is that as long as you use Titanium objects as "building blocks" to make your own objects, they'll run across platforms, because the base objects run across platforms.

Convenience Functions

In any programming language, you'll often need to do the same thing over and over. More specifically, you'll need to use some functionality over and over that probably uses a similar set of code. This is a good opportunity to make a convenience function that combines those lines of code into a single object, such as a JavaScript function.

Let's take writing a file as an example. It's fairly simple, but it does require a few lines of code that aren't necessarily intuitive or simple to remember. The Titanium code that would be required to write a file is as follows:

```
var file = "";

var filename ="output.txt";
var filedata = "I need to save this to a file";

if (TiR.Filesystem.isExternalStoragePresent()  ) {
    file = Titanium.Filesystem.getFile(Ti.Filesystem.externalStorageDirectory,
    filename);
} else {
    file = Titanium.Filesystem.getFile(Ti.Filesystem.applicationDataDirectory,
    filename);
}

if (!file.exists) {
    file.createFile();
}

file.write(filedata);
```

This isn't super complicated. It starts with a simple check to see whether a file exists, and if not, creates it and then writes out the data. This is a situation that you'll likely find yourself in over and over again. So instead of having 10+ lines all over the place doing a few base Titanium commands, why not put it into a function such as the following?

```
function fileWrite(filename,datatowrite) {
    var file = "";
    if (TiR.Filesystem.isExternalStoragePresent()  ) {
      file = Titanium.Filesystem.getFile(Ti.Filesystem.externalStorageDirectory,
      filename);
    } else {
      file = Titanium.Filesystem.getFile(Ti.Filesystem.applicationDataDirectory,
      filename);
    };
    if (!file.exists) {
      file.createFile();
    }
    file.write(filedata);
}
```

This allows you to accomplish the task with a single line of code, such as the following:

```
fileWrite("output.txt","I need to save this to a file");
```

Another good reason to do this, which will also benefit others around you developing Titanium apps, is that it simplifies a bit of weird syntax. When I first needed to write a file, it was a bit confusing. I was expecting something like "create" or "open" to initialize the file and then a function to write it. The syntax for Titanium makes you "get" the file first, instead.

As you can see in the code sample, you do a "get" on the filename and the file location, which returns a file object. By using the `exists` property, you can see whether the file exists. If not, you issue a `createFile` on the file object, which just seemed a little odd to me. Creating a `fileWrite` function makes things easier down the road, as you don't have to remember anything other than the parameters to send the function.

Creating a custom function also allows you to do different things based on the platform. For instance, on Android you can write files either to the storage on the phone or to the SD card, if there is one. On iOS, your only option is to write to the storage on the phone itself as there is no external storage.

A function like this could isolate the programmer from this by doing one thing for iOS and another for Android. Instead, the functions do different things based on what platform it is running on. It also helps protect your apps against changes in the Titanium API. If changes in Titanium's API break your app, you can handle the change in your compatibility layer and not have to rewrite sections of code scattered all over your app.

Creating convenience functions is yet another way to use JavaScript creatively and help you extend the Titanium framework in a way that makes it easier for you or your company to work with it. It's also a great way to encapsulate functionality that would be needed across a lot of apps.

Titanium Modules and Their Uses

One of the nicest things about Titanium is that from early on, Appcelerator incorporated the ability to write a "standalone" module that can be integrated into any mobile app. These modules expose native functionality of the device they are running on that might not be included with Titanium out of the box. To some extent this is a developer's "ace in the hole" when deciding whether Titanium makes sense for your project. The good news is that you can write your own modules. The bad news is that modules have to be written using 100% native tools and native languages. For iOS modules, this means you have to write your module in Objective-C, whereas for Android you have to write it in Java.

There are two main reasons why you'd want to write a module:

1. You want to access native functionality of the device, such as the camera, geolocation, or other features, that isn't already exposed by the Titanium Framework.

2. You want to write an interface to an outside system, such as Facebook or Dropbox, that is involved enough that others would want to have a plug-and-play solution. This isn't restricted to consumer-facing apps. There could be an enterprise app that needed to access a back-office system such as SAP or Oracle. If you have the skills in-house, you might want to write a module that would do the heavy lifting and provide an easy way to access this data.

How to Write a Module

When you want to write your own custom module, you need to know how to do that in that native language for the platform that you want your module to run on, along with the platform's tools. Naturally, this book can't convey all that background, but I can get you started with the Titanium-specific issues.

Once you know the environment of the mobile platform, writing a module is fairly straightforward. For iOS, you enter some commands on the command line that create an Xcode project, which you can then use to write your functionality in Objective-C. In a nutshell, when you want to write your own Titanium module, you have to run some scripts to create a project for you that you can put your code in.

This "mini" framework gives you a standard Titanium module that you are used to working with along with the code for your module. This gives you a familiar place to work on your module and test it within a Titanium app.

When you write a module for Titanium, you start to realize the work that went into the product. If you want to write modules in Titanium that work on multiple platforms, you'll need to write one module for each platform you want it to run on. That's why many times you can find a module for Titanium written by third parties outside of their marketplace, but only for one platform.

I came across a barcode scanning module for Android written by a company that needed the functionality themselves but couldn't find it. They had no choice but to write the module themselves, or just go without. The point here is that they wrote it only for Android because that was their immediate need.

Modules are available in the Titanium Marketplace to give you access to Dropbox files, handle PayPal payments, allow In-App purchases on iOS, and deal with other tasks that could take a long time to handle from scratch. The best way to see what modules are available is to simply go to the Titanium Marketplace and see what modules might be there that you could make use of.

Many of the modules are available for free, for a free trial, or for a relatively low price, either monthly or as a one-time payment. Once you try a few out, I think you'll agree that Titanium modules are a great way to get some advanced functionality into your app, quickly and easily.

The time and knowledge for writing functionality for both iOS and Android is a bit of a rare bird outside of Appcelerator. They have in-house resources for both iOS and Android, so it's not such a stretch for them to support both platforms. For an individual developer, or even a small development company, it's a much bigger deal. So, when you find Titanium modules "in the wild" don't be surprised if they're developed for a single platform.

Although a step-by-step tutorial on writing a Titanium module is out of the scope of this book, I recommend this iOS Module Development Guide (*https://wiki.appcelera tor.org/display/guides/iOS+Module+Development+Guide*).

Titanium Mobile Marketplace

The Titanium Mobile Marketplace is a way for developers to create and sell modules that they have created for Titanium and allows other developers to use those modules in their apps. Titanium modules are a great way to get functionality into your app without having to worry about all the details that go along with it.

A barcode scanning module is a great example of this. Without a Titanium module, you would have to do a lot of coding yourself that might not be enjoyable or even easy to do. Since Titanium makes it easy to develop apps in JavaScript, it's quite possible that a Titanium developer wouldn't have the skills necessary to build a native module themselves.

That's where the mobile marketplace really shines. This brings together developers who can MAKE Titanium Modules with developers who want to USE Titanium modules in their app. Using the barcode scanning example, I integrated my own Objective-C code in an app I was working on to create barcode scanning functionality. It was interesting to do to a certain degree, but there was plenty of frustration to go along with it.

Being able to drop in a module, reference it, and call a method with a few lines of JavaScript just can't be beat to quickly get functionality into your app. If the module you're looking at runs across both iOS and Android, so much the better.

Using a Titanium Module

Even though a tutorial on *writing* a Titanium module isn't in the scope of this book, it's certainly worthwhile to show you how you'd *use* a Titanium module in your project. I have a nice appreciation for Titanium modules myself because I've been on both sides of that fence.

One of the first apps I wrote (using PhoneGap) was an app to provide barcode scanning functionality available in the App Store under the name Scan For All. I was using PhoneGap to create an iOS app that would scan barcodes. Since PhoneGap didn't have this functionality out of the box, I had to find an Objective-C module that would provide this functionality and somehow give my app the needed features.

I was able to find a library fairly easily that was based on the ZXing ("Zebra Crossing") implementation. Lucky for me, there was also a sample project in Xcode that gave me a good frame of reference for using the code within Xcode, which of course was where my PhoneGap project was located. After quite a bit of trial and error (mostly error), I was able to get the ZXing Xcode project integrated into my app as a library that I was able to call via Objective-C code. The Objective-C part was a little easier for me since, before I took on bringing in this code as a library, I had written quite a bit of Objective-C in order to get access to native UI components instead of having to redo them in HTML5.

Now that I had the library in Xcode, I wanted to have an easy way to call it via JavaScript. When I was extending PhoneGap to allow access to native UI components, I had seen how the JavaScript-to-Native bridge was set up programmatically, so I was able to write some code that would allow me to call the scanning library in Xcode and return the scanned information back to the calling JavaScript function.

As the saying goes, "whatever doesn't kill you makes you stronger," so I guess I'm stronger for this ordeal, but I would have been glad to have an easier way around all this multi-language work. Recently I was in a similar situation, writing a mobile app using Titanium instead of PhoneGap, and needed to have some barcode reading functionality built in. This time, however, it was a much different experience.

There are basically three steps in using a Titanium Module: adding the module to your project filesystem, configuring your project to include the module, and calling the module from your JavaScript code. As I describe how to add a module, I'll be doing it from the perspective of an Android app, but it's 100% the same process for iOS.

Adding the Module

The first step to using a module in your Titanium project is to copy the code into your project filesystem. When you download the module from Titanium's Marketplace, the resulting files will look something like Figure 7-1 in your *downloads* folder.

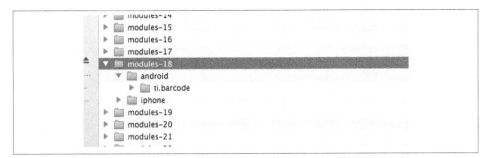

Figure 7-1. Downloading a Titanium module

In this case, the folder holding the barcode scanning module is located in the *modules-18* directory. Unfortunately, when you download a module, the installer just creates a new folder bearing a name that begins with *module-*, so after a few tries (18 in my case), you end up with quite a few *modules* directories. In every *module* directory, the next level down will be the platforms it supports. You'll see *android* for the Android-related modules and *iphone* for the iOS-related modules. So far, so good.

What you need to do now is move one or more of the platform-specific folders into the actual Titanium project. The way to do this is quite simply copying the folder containing the module's folder (*ti.barcode* in this case) into the platform folder (*android* in this case) in the filesystem for the Titanium project. As you can see in Figure 7-2, the *ti.barcode* folder is going into the *modules/android* directory in the Titanium project.

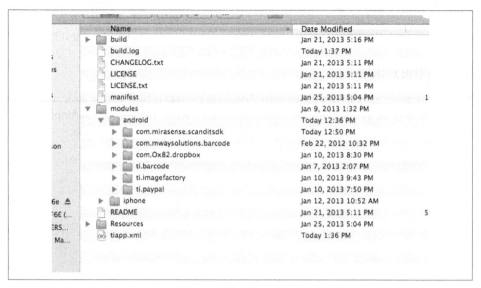

Figure 7-2. The filesystem for a Titanium Mobile Project with a module directory added (ti.barcode)

Referencing the Module

Now that you've added the actual files for the module, you need to configure your project to know about these files so that it can reference them at runtime. You can do this pretty easily in Titanium Studio under Modules (Figure 7-3). You can easily see which modules are currently enabled by looking at the Modules section in Titanium Studio.

While viewing modules, you can add another module by clicking on the plus sign (+) to the right of the module names. When you click on that, a pop-up will appear that shows you all the modules that Titanium Studio "knows" about, typically all the modules that are in the filesystem under the top-level *modules* folder (Figure 7-4). This allows you to store modules in the filesystem without necessarily including them in every project.

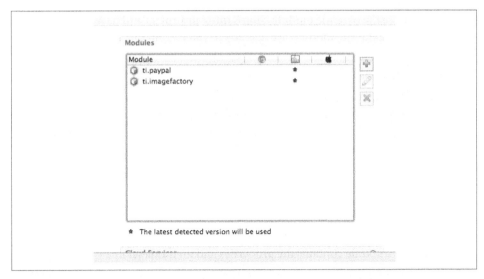

Figure 7-3. List of modules that are currently included in the project

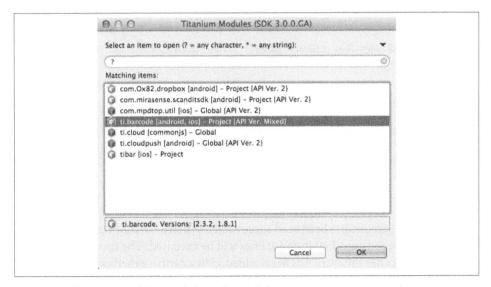

Figure 7-4. Dialog to add a module to the Mobile Project

Any modules you add to the module list in Titanium Studio will be included in the final project when it's built. Each module contains platform-specific files that are included when the project is built for each targeted platform. There are also some JavaScript interfaces set up that allow you to call the module from your Titanium JavaScript code.

Now that we have the barcode module copied into our project and have configured our project to know about the module, we're ready to call it from our code.

Calling a Module from Titanium Code

Titanium is all about proxy objects. When you create a Titanium button, for example, what you're really creating is a JavaScript proxy object that knows how to talk to the native button. What happens with modules is the same thing, except that the proxy object points to an object written by an outside developer.

What you need to do, therefore, is create this proxy object with a line of JavaScript like this:

```
bcode.Barcode = require('ti.barcode');
```

This creates a new JavaScript object that is a proxy to the native object that resides in the module. The module contains the properties and methods set up by the author. You can now access these properties and methods via the JavaScript proxy.

Here is a small code listing that shows how easily you would use the Barcode object to scan a barcode:

```
bcode.Barcode = require('ti.barcode');

bcode.Barcode.addEventListener('success', function (e) {
  alert(e);
});

bcode.Barcode.capture({
    animate: true,
    showCancel: true,
    showRectangle: true,
    keepOpen: false
});
```

On the first line, require sets up a JavaScript proxy object as we discussed before. The next three lines assign an event handler to the "success" event that the barcode object will fire when a barcode has been read successfully. When a barcode has been read, the anonymous function specified in those lines will be executed. The final block of code, which runs right after the event listener is added, calls a capture method on the barcode object. This opens up a window that shows the scanning overlay to make it easier for the user to know how to position the barcode within the view. The user presumably will then position the device over the barcode and press a button to scan it, whereupon the "success" routine is called and the scanning view closes.

As you can see, using a Titanium Module is fairly straightforward and gives you an easy way to integrate functionality written by third-party developers. This gives you an easy way to integrate what could be complicated functionality into your app very easily.

Appcelerator Cloud Services

Another cool features of Titanium that was recently introduced is Appcelerator Cloud Services (ACS). These are a series of web services included with the Titanium environment. When used, it includes the necessary modules in the mobile runtime binary so it all "just works."

Any good mobile app lives and dies on the data that it can pull from a web service, display, and possibly send back to another web service. The majority of corporate mobile apps will have to use data retrieved from a backend service, and many consumer apps make use of web services as well. This is one of the harder tasks to take on during the evolution of a mobile app. You need to figure out where to have the services hosted, what language to code them in, and how you want to account for a large number of hits, if your app starts getting a lot of use.

This is where ACS can add value and take a lot of variables out of the equation. ACS is a series of hosted services on a robust, scalable environment that can handle the traffic that your app might send to it. ACS as a whole is officially still in beta right now, and the API is subject to change. As such, we won't get into a detailed discussion about it. It's a good point to keep in mind when comparing frameworks, though, as this could be a large check in the "pro" column.

ACS offers services such as email, push notifications, chats, checkins, photos, places, posts, etc. In addition to being able to call ACS from your mobile app, you can also simply call it as a web service via standard REST calls. This allows you to make use of ACS even outside of your mobile app. Since ACS is still classified as beta now, use this link (*http://docs.appcelerator.com/titanium/latest/#!/api/Titanium.Cloud*) to get the most up-to-date information about ACS and how it can make your app great.

CHAPTER 8

Titanium App Storage

All mobile apps need to store some data to be useful. If there is a file or something else that the user will need more than once or twice, it makes sense to store it locally. This will make it immediately available next time the app is run, and more importantly, if there is no cell service available. Designing an app to work even if there is no cell signal makes it that much more valuable. This is where caching data plays a big part. If the network is available, data can be downloaded, and if not, a cached version can be used. HTML5, for instance, provides a "cache manifest" to address this need. Since Titanium creates native apps, it can't use the cache manifest, but it's quite possible to create a download function that maintains a cache of previously downloaded items and uses the cached version if it's available.

Local File Storage

One way to store data onto a mobile device is to put it in a regular old filesystem file. This is a pretty convenient way to store data, especially text or JSON data. Writing to a file doesn't require much setup, and both the writing and the reading back are quick and easy. Also, on Android devices, the external storage makes a good place to store files that another app might need to read. This is impossible on iOS devices, though, as there is no external storage. Of course you can still write files to the iOS filesystem, it's just not on an external SD card and an app can only read the files in its own sandbox storage area.

Here is a quick example of how you might write data to the filesystem running on iOS or Android:

```
file = Titanium.Filesystem.getFile(Ti.Filesystem.applicationDataDirectory);
if (!file.exists) {
    file.createFile();
}
```

```
bolSuccess = file.write(filedata);
Ti.API.debug("file written...native path = " + file.nativePath);
```

One of the strengths of writing to files is that it's easy to save some data to a simple text file with just a few lines of code. You don't have to be familiar with any kind of database operations or how to connect to a database at runtime, how to insert rows, etc.

Database Storage

A lightweight database can be supremely useful on a mobile device. These devices now have the power to drive a lightweight database that doesn't need to have tons of data in it. There are two main reasons why you'd want to use a database in your mobile app:

1. You have data that changes a lot or is variable. A good example of this might be a task list or a barcode scanner where you need to keep track of items scanned or to-do items. As new items are added, a database is a great place to store them.

2. You need to retrieve the data in a variety of ways. One of the big strengths of a database is its ability to retrieve a variety of fields, sorted and grouped as you specify. Because the database is compiled and optimized, retrieval is generally fast. To use text fields for the same operation would be a huge mistake, as all the processing would be done in JavaScript and all the data would need to be sorted. It would be a huge time drain compared to simply issuing a SELECT statement on the database.

A bit of a downside is that there is some setup and some knowledge involved in using a database, even a simple one. Here's a quick example of how you'd create your database and get it ready to install rows. SQL is simply wrapped by JavaScript functions that execute it:

```
var db = Titanium.Database.open('mydb');

db.execute('CREATE TABLE IF NOT EXISTS DATABASETEST  (ID INTEGER, NAME TEXT)');
db.execute('DELETE FROM DATABASETEST');

db.execute('INSERT INTO DATABASETEST (ID, NAME ) VALUES(?,?)',1,'Name 1');
db.execute('INSERT INTO DATABASETEST (ID, NAME ) VALUES(?,?)',2,'Name 2');
db.execute('INSERT INTO DATABASETEST (ID, NAME ) VALUES(?,?)',3,'Name 3');
db.execute('INSERT INTO DATABASETEST (ID, NAME ) VALUES(?,?)',4,'Name 4');
var updateName = 'I was updated';
var updateId = 4;
db.execute('UPDATE DATABASETEST SET NAME = ? WHERE ID = ?',
    updateName, updateId);
db.execute('UPDATE DATABASETEST SET NAME = "I was updated too" WHERE ID = 2');
db.execute('DELETE FROM DATABASETEST WHERE ID = ?',1);

Titanium.API.info('JUST INSERTED, rowsAffected = ' + db.rowsAffected);
Titanium.API.info('JUST INSERTED, lastInsertRowId = ' + db.lastInsertRowId);
```

```
var rows = db.execute('SELECT * FROM DATABASETEST');
Titanium.API.info('ROW COUNT = ' + rows.getRowCount());
```

Titanium makes it easy to use SQLite databases via some fairly simple API calls.

You get a top-level database object by opening a database via a database name; in this example, it's mydb. This creates a database if none is present, and simply opens the existing database if it is there. This only creates or opens the database. It doesn't do anything other than open the existing database or create it if it doesn't exist.

OK, so you've now got a handle to a database, now what? Well, you need to send SQL statements to the database instance. These cause the database to process your request and return a message back. If there are errors in the SQL statement, then this is indicated in the response.

For all the functionality that can be accessed in a SQL database, there are only a few methods that can be called...three to be precise:

execute
> Runs an SQL statement and returns the result.

close
> Closes the database and releases resources from memory. Once closed, the database instance is no longer valid and should not be used unless you reconnect. On iOS, it also closes all Titanium.Database.ResultSet instances that exist.

remove
> Removes the database files for this instance from disk.

 This is a destructive operation and cannot be reversed. All data in the database will be lost; use with caution.

Ninety-nine percent of the time, you'll just use the database object's execute function to run commands against the database.

rowsAffected returns the number of rows affected by the last query run via the most recent execute method call. When you use a select statement to populate a Result Set, you'll be able to tell how many matching rows were found by looking at this property. However, some operations, such as a delete or an update, don't return any results, but just update the database. This is when the rowsAffected really comes in handy. Any kind of operation on the database will update this property, which will save you from jumping through some SQL hoops to find out how many rows were affected by a SQL operation.

ResultSets

Some database operations can be done with a simple execute of a SQL statement to update some rows, insert some data, etc. Other times you'll want to SELECT some rows and get them back as objects that you can iterate through and use in some way. This is exactly what a ResultSet is for.

The syntax for creating a ResultSet is very straightforward. Previously, we saw how to open a database and execute some SQL statements against it. Now, we'll use that same database connection to populate a ResultSet with an SQL statement that returns data.

For this example, let's assume that we have a database table called *table1* with the following structure and data in it:

ID	First name	Last name	Order Number
1	John	Anderson	127634
2	Jane	Anderson	872838
3	Jerry	Seinfeld	888888
4	Homer	Simpson	792832
5	Marge	Simpson	983938

Then you could populate a ResultSet with a command such as this:

```
var rows = db.execute('SELECT * from table1 order');
```

Now you have the results in the variable rows, which you can loop through and view using methods of the ResultSet. The ResultSet always considers one row to be the current row, and returns information about that row. Some of the methods you'll be using the most are:

fieldByName

> Returns the value of a field in the current row. The name is the column name assigned in the database.

next

> Advances to the next row in the ResultSet. By using repeated calls to next, you can iterate through all the rows in the ResultSet and inspect any of the field values using fieldByName.

> The next method will return a value of true when there was actually another row to advance to, or false if you are at the end of the ResultSet and there are no more rows.

`close`

> Closes the `ResultSet` and releases memory and any other resources associated with it. This is important to do. Many UI elements will automatically be destroyed when the containing window is closed, but database resources need to be explicitly closed so that the resources used by it are properly released.

There are other properties and methods offered by the `ResultSet`, but these three are the main ones you'll be using to retrieve rows from a database and process the results. With a handful of methods and properties on both the `Database` and `ResultSet` objects, they can give your app quite a bit of power to handle complex data structures.

With great power, however, comes great responsibility. This is certainly an area where testing on a device is key. If your app is going to use database functionality more than a bit, it's important to test on as many devices as possible. Running a simulator on a desktop or laptop computer can easily give you a false sense of security in terms of performance, and running on a device can reveal problems that require rethinking your use of the database.

Test early and test often as you develop your app so that you can see whether your use of a database is going to adversely affect your app. There is no worse feeling than thinking you are finished with an app and then testing it on a device for the first time and finding out that it runs poorly on a real device.

On-device databases can give you a lot of power in storing data locally in a way that gives you flexibility in storing, retrieving, and sorting to give your app users a great experience. Relational databases can either be used very simply or in a way that makes use of all the power that they have to offer. What we've done in this chapter shows you how to use a SQLite database in your Titanium app. Using the `db.execute()` method allows you to use any command that SQLite has to offer.

A full discussion on SQLite would fill up an entire book, but you can get more information in *Using SQLite* by Jay A. Kreibich (O'Reilly, 2010) and other sources.

CHAPTER 9

Distribution Methods

An app is not worth much if all it does is run on your simulator, or perhaps on your own USB-connected device. The point of apps is having other people use them, and ideally having other people pay for them. Although we're not going to go into detail on these different methods, it's good to touch on them so that you can have some idea of the pros and cons of distributing your apps in the different ways available.

Apple's App Store

Although this wasn't the first online "place" to allow you to purchase (I purchased some BREW-based apps on an old cell phone I had via the service provider) it is by all means the most popular, most profitable, and most talked about. When iOS 2.0 came out with a cute little "App Store" icon, I dare say no one, even at Apple, had a feeling for the impact this little thing would have on the world. Although the built-in apps are nice and functional, they aren't why you love your mobile device. It's the games and other apps that are developed by developers and software companies that make you check to make sure you have it before you leave the house.

Getting your app in the App Store grants you access to millions of customers just a single tap away from buying your app, and in the process giving you some money. It's a pretty great deal for independent developers especially who can build an app, upload it, and let the world buy it, or buy it and give a review. The flip side of this is that Apple decides what can and can't be in the App Store. Deal with it or don't submit anything.

Titanium lowers the bar quite a bit for creating an app that can get into the App Store, and allows you to develop apps more quickly than using native tools. Even though it's quicker, it still uses native controls and looks like a native app. Big companies are using Titanium to build very public apps.

Custom B2B Apps

Custom B2B (Business to Business) is a subcategory of apps that are in Apple's App Store. It's hard to tell how popular it is because those apps aren't available for viewing by the general public. By enrolling in Apple's Volume Purchase Program, businesses are able to buy apps in volume, making it easier to purchase and distribute paid apps for their employees. The Volume Purchase Program is available in the United States only.

In addition to offering apps from the App Store, the Volume Purchase Program enables businesses to buy custom B2B apps developed for their unique needs. Businesses can work with third-party app developers and business partners to procure these custom B2B apps securely and privately through the program. Custom B2B apps are built to address a unique business need, and therefore are not available to the general public for purchase. Custom B2B apps are designed to provide tailored solutions that extend the possibilities of iPhone and iPad in business. For example, a custom B2B app could offer:

- A customized user interface, including company logo or branding
- Unique features or capabilities specific to a business process or workflow
- Extra privacy protection to handle sensitive data
- A specific configuration to meet the customer's server/back-office environment or IT environment
- Features targeted to a limited audience, such as a business partner, dealer, or franchise

Businesses can buy custom B2B apps from developers in a private transaction through the Volume Purchasing Program. The minimum price for a custom B2B app is $9.99.

Apple's Enterprise Distribution

Another mode of distribution from Apple is not much more than a file you download, but in the right scenario it's pretty powerful. What I'm talking about is Apple's Enterprise Distribution program/profile. This is geared to companies (any one with a DUNS number) that want to distribute internally-developed apps to their employees for their use on iOS devices. These are not visible to the world, unless some company does the unwise thing of putting these apps on a server that is public facing and has no security on it. Apps compiled with an Enterprise Distribution profile can be installed on any device in the world. You won't get paid for it, and you won't get automatic alerts that an update is available, but it can be a powerful asset.

The main cool thing about Enterprise Distribution is that Apple has no control over the content in the apps that you distribute. You can literally compile your apps, put a few files on a web server, and voilà, you've set up your own little App Store. Three files are needed to do this: an HTML file that provides the user interface, the *.ipa* file, and

---

the *.plist* file or property list generated when you compiled and shared the app. This is very simple from the end user's point of view. He simply opens up the Safari browser on his mobile device and puts in the URL of the HTML file. Mobile Safari displays this as it would any web page with a link to install the app. When that link is tapped, the link sends some info to the phone that causes it to download and install the *.ipa* file.

The basic process of distributing apps them becomes more like deploying a web app than a native app for iOS. Let's walk through the process so you can get a feel for how simple it is. Let's start at the point of having your app finished and now you need to deploy it.

Select "Distribute to App Store" from Titanium's Deployment menu (Figure 9-1). You won't be going to the App Store, but this is the option that generates an IPA from your code, which is what we need to do. Once we get into the next step, we can select a distribution license that will embed the appropriate provisioning profile onto the device.

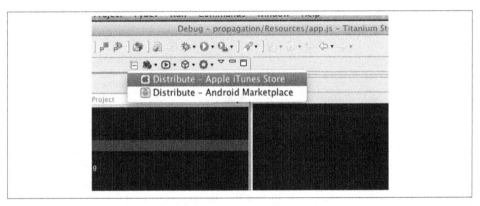

Figure 9-1. Selecting "Distribute to App Store"

Once you select this option, another dialog box will come up to let us indicate this is something for Enterprise Distribution (Figure 9-2).

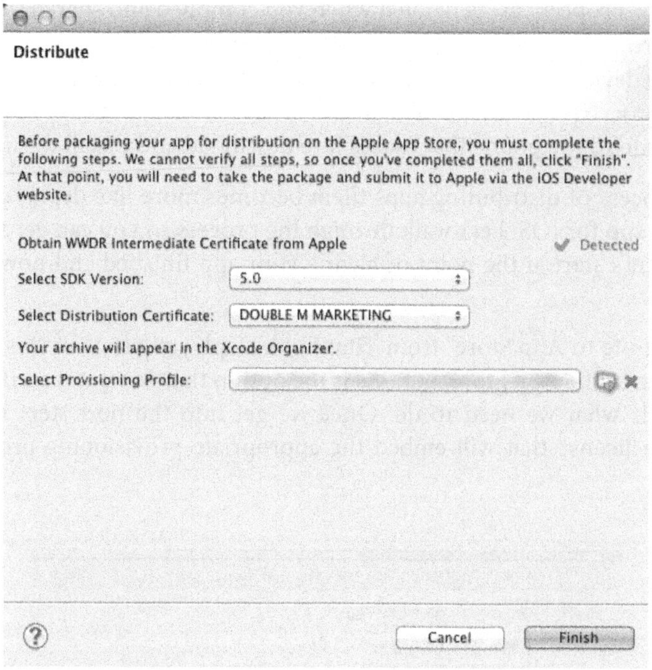

Figure 9-2. Distribute dialog

This dialog box gives you the option to select the Distribution Certificate and the Provisioning Profile you want to use. These two items embed information into the app so it basically knows whether it should run on a device or not. When you put an app into the App Store, it contains information that basically says "I came from the App Store, so run on any device." When someone clicks the Buy button, the app is downloaded onto the device and information is recorded at Apple so they know that you purchased an app on your iTunes account.

When you compile an app for Enterprise Distribution, it includes a copy of your Enterprise Provisioning profile in the app. Enterprise-distributed apps are set up to run on any number of devices. The onus is on the company using the Enterprise certs to make sure they don't allow more than 5,000 employees access to the app. That's the only limitation.

Every time an app is distributed using an Enterprise cert, it checks with Apple servers to make sure the cert is still valid, and that the app should still run. It doesn't do this every single time it runs, but caches the information for a few days, maybe a week. The point is that the app will check frequently to make sure the cert is valid and it should still run.

If an Enterprise violates Apple's terms of service, Apple is in a position to revoke their certificate, and the apps built and distributed using it would stop working soon after. This is the incentive for Enterprise to play by the rules. But I digress—back to distributing our Enterprise app.

Once you click the Finish button on the Distribute dialog, Titanium goes to work building your app and including your Enterprise Provisioning Profile so that it will run when downloaded onto a device outside of the App Store. When Titanium is finished building the IPA, you'll be able to see it in Xcode's Organizer window. We'll finish the process there.

When the build is done, you should see Xcode's Organizer window come up automatically (Figure 9-3).

Figure 9-3. Organizer

Now you'll simply need to select the Share button, which will export the *.ipa* file into a standalone file that you'll be able to use to distribute the app internally. When you do that, you'll get a popup that will let you re-sign the file with different certificates, but normally you would just select "Don't re-sign" at this point (Figure 9-4). The app is signed when you build it, so you don't have to re-sign here.

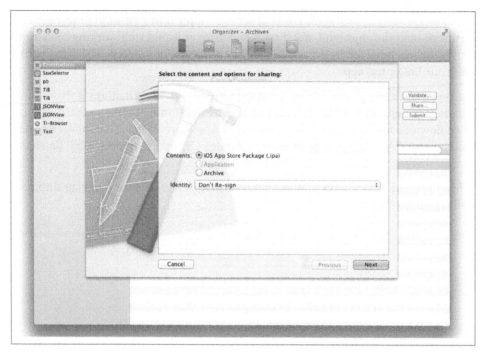

Figure 9-4. Don't re-sign the app when it is distributed internally

You'll then be prompted to select a destination to save the file, and options to include parameters for Enterprise Distribution. If you select this checkbox, it will open up several fields that you'll need to fill in. Those fields include the following:

Application URL
> The URL where the IPA will be stored. It can either be a publicly available URL or an internal URL. In any event, the entire URL including the IPA name should be entered here.

Title
> The title of the app that will be shown below the app icon.

Subtitle
> An optional field for the subtitle for the app.

Large Image URL
> An optional field for a large version of the app icon.

Small Image URL
> An optional field for the URL that will appear only while the app is being installed. Once the app is installed, the icon from the app bundle will be used as the icon.

Add Shine Effect to Images
A checkbox that will let the device know whether it should add shine effects to the large and small app icons.

Once you fill out this form, Xcode will create two files at the destination location provided:

app.ipa
The app file that will be downloaded onto a device.

app.plist
A property list that contains information about where the app is located.

Now all that remains is to create an HTML file that will be placed at the same location as the *.ipa* and *.plist* files on the web server where users will download the app. The HTML file that needs to be created is as follows:

```
<meta name = "viewport" content = "width = device-width">
<meta name = "viewport" content = "initial-scale = 1.0">
<href="itms-services://?action=download-manifest&url=http://<servername>/OTAT-
est2/app.plist">Enterprise App</a>
```

This very basic web page allows the app to be downloaded onto a device. Assuming the page is called *index.html*, you'd go to the URL:

```
http://<servername>/otatest2/index.html
```

This would then bring up the `itms-services://` link in the web page. You'll notice that the protocol (normally `http://`) in the URL is a little different. iOS devices allow special URLs to be set up that will initiate an action on the phone instead of going to an actual URL. This is one of them. This URL basically tells iTunes on the iOS device to handle the URL instead of having Safari handle it.

After the user clicks on the link, iTunes on the device takes over using the information provided in the link. The `action` parameter tells it to download the manifest file indicated in the `url` parameter. It downloads the plist and processes it. The content of the plist is as follows:

```
<?xml version="1.0" encoding="UTF-8"?>
<!DOCTYPE plist PUBLIC "-//Apple//DTD PLIST 1.0//EN" "http://www.apple.com/DTDs/
PropertyList-1.0.dtd">
<plist version="1.0">
<dict>
  <key>items</key>
  <array>
    <dict>
      <key>assets</key>
      <array>
        <dict>
          <key>kind</key>
          <string>software-package</string>
```

```
          <key>url</key>
          <string>http://serverurl/pathtoapp/app.ipa</string>
        </dict>
      </array>
      <key>metadata</key>
      <dict>
        <key>bundle-identifier</key>
        <string>com.mpdtop.crossplatform</string>
        <key>bundle-version</key>
        <string>1.0</string>
        <key>kind</key>
        <string>software</string>
        <key>title</key>
        <string>Mobile App</string>
      </dict>
    </dict>
  </array>
</dict>
</plist>
```

This has all the information that iTunes on the device needs to download and install the app. The most important piece of information is the URL showing where the *.ipa* file is located. All the other version information must be the same as in the app. If you need to update the app later on, you'd need to replace both the *.ipa* as well as the *.plist* file so the information is in sync between the two.

Now anyone who wants to run the app can simply enter the URL, click on a link in an email, or something else convenient, and the app will be downloaded onto their device.

Depending on how fancy you want to get with the download HTML page, you can make it look very similar to the appearance of the official App Store. Not that you want to make anyone think that they are downloading from the App Store, but it's always nice to mimic the look and feel a bit so that users understand what's going on.

Android's Marketplace

Android Marketplace is more of the wild west when it comes to what can and can't go into their store. Pretty much anything you can build can get into the marketplace. I've uploaded apps that showed up in the marketplace about 15 minutes later. So you don't have to worry about as much control being put on you in terms of what you can put in it and what you can't.

Even though there is significantly more latitude with what you can put in the marketplace, there are also situations where you might not want the world to see your app or know that it's out there. In a similar way to Apple's Enterprise distribution, you can simply put your *.apk* file on a web server, and you're in business with your own little marketplace. You won't make money, but if you want to keep your app private, this might be something to think about.

All your users need is to open up a web browser on their device and plug in the URL to it and the *.apk* file will be downloaded and installed. The only catch I've seen with this setup is on Android phones from some carriers who shall remain nameless (but I can offer its initials: AT&T) where sometimes you can't install apps this way. Some carriers modify the build for the phones sold through their stores so that this feature simply isn't available. You can still install your apps on a device via USB cable and enable USB debugging, but no over-the-air installs outside of Google Play.

But, if your phone or table supports it, go forth and distribute apps. I've been able to install Titanium-built apps on Android phones, smaller tablets (like Galaxy Tab), and Honeycomb-based tablets (such as Acer).

CHAPTER 10

API Reference

As with any library, Titanium offers an integrated API that gives you access to the features it has to offer. The Titanium API is organized into several different namespaces, which are fairly self explanatory. For instance, UI components exist in the `Titanium.UI` namespace and can be invoked as `Titanium.UIxxx`.

When referring to Titanium methods and constants, `Ti` can be used instead of `Titanium`. So `Ti.UI.createTableView` is the same as `Titanium.UI.createTableView`.

The namespaces in this chapter range from fairly complex and full, such as the UI namespace, down to ones that have only a method or two. These namespaces also contain constants, which are JavaScript variables that cannot be changed and that have a fixed meaning that's useful in programming with that namespace's methods. Even though many times you need to look them up in the reference material, it's easier to use something like `Titanium.UI.iPhone.TableViewStyle.GROUPED` than 234587923. Furthermore, if Titanium changes the definition of a constant, your code can be recompiled and still work without being rewritten.

Condensing Your Code

It's a little time consuming to have to remember the full namespaces of methods and constants. For instance, if you want to make a table view with a style of GROUPED, you need to write:

```
tableview = Ti.UI.createTableView({
    style:Titanium.UI.iPhone.TableViewStyle.GROUPED
});
```

Since I don't have a photographic memory, I've built up a file with some convenience functions and some of my own constants for common activities. I then include this file in any of my projects and all my time-saving functions are at my fingertips. A sample of the file looks like this:

```
        tableStyle = {};
        ...
        tableStyle.GROUPED = Titanium.UI.iPhone.TableViewStyle.GROUPED;
```

This allows me to create a grouped table view with the following line:

```
    tableview = Ti.UI.createTableView({style:tableStyle.GROUPED})
```

which for me is worlds easier to remember than the constant in the Titanium API. This is just a small example of how you can use different aspects of JavaScript to make your coding easier and more productive in Titanium.

The rest of this chapter lists some namespaces in Titanium and illustrates how to use some of them. It's obviously beyond the scope of this book to provide a comprehensive reference for all of these functions. What you will find is a 30-second "elevator pitch" for these API functions that should help you understand the purpose of the functions, without a detailed explanation of each one.

Titanium

This is the top-level entry point into the Titanium API, and equivalent to Ti. As the top-level entry point, it will appear all over your code. The Titanium module provides the Titanium Mobile API, allowing developers to access native features of each target environment. Currently, the Android, iOS, and Mobile Web (beta) environments are supported.

This namespace doesn't have methods of its own, but does define some constants that let you know such things as the version of Titanium you are using and data about the build of Titanium.

Again, it's good to remember that Titanium is equivalent to "Ti," so instead of `Titanium.UI.createButton`, use `Ti.UI.createButton`.

Titanium.API

This contains methods to output messages to the system log. This provides a way of logging information to the console during the execution of your app in debugging mode. There are several different methods representing messages with different severities. In the Titanium console, you can choose the levels of severity displayed, depending on what you might be debugging at the time.

Thus, you can log information that is simply helpful, such as "app started" or "app finished" using `Ti.API.trace()`. Another level up in severity is `Ti.API.debug()`, and so on. Here are some examples of each method:

```
Ti.API.trace("uploading the file");
Ti.API.debug("this is just some handy information");
Ti.API.info("running some part of the code");
Ti.API.warn("something bad is about to happen");
Ti.API.error("something bad just happened");
```

As innocent-looking and simple as these functions are, they will probably become some of your best friends. Other than using the step-through debugger in Titanium Studio, this is the best way to see what your app is doing when running.

Before testing your app in Titanium Studio, select the minimum level of severity you want to see in the console. For instance, if you select Info in the simulator (Figure 10-1), trace and debug log events won't show up, but info, warning, and error messages will. If you select Error, nothing but entries logged with Ti.API.error() will be shown on the console. This gives you a handy way to log lots of information and then tune up or down the amount of information you want to see while testing.

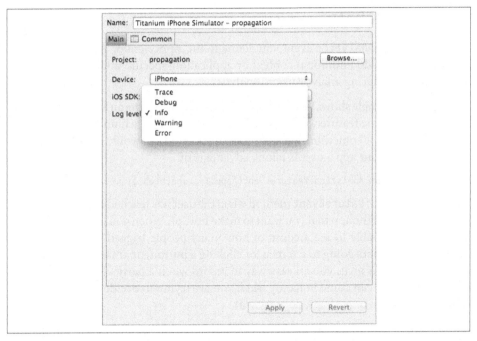

Figure 10-1. Setting the log level you want to see in the console when running your app

Titanium.Accelerometer

These modules contain methods and properties for using the device's accelerometer. The accelerometer allows you to sense orientations changes in the phone, such as when the user turns it from landscape to portrait mode or places it face down. Here is a trivial use that just displays the current position:

```
Titanium.Accelerometer.addEventListener('update',function(e)
{
    Ti.API.debug("accelerometer - x:"+e.x+",y:"+e.y+",z:"+e.z);
});
```

As you move the device around, the 'update' event will be fired as appropriate (several times a second). When it fires, you'll receive coordinates that represent the current position of the device.

Titanium.Analytics

This transmits an Analytics event you define to the Appcelerator Analytics product. It can be used to add additional context or application-specific information that can then be accessed during analysis using Analytics.

The following example shows how to send a featureEvent during an application session to indicate that some feature was triggered or used by the user whom you would like to track. This would be something like app.geo.checkin, which would allow you to track what features of your app a user is taking advantage of:

```
Titanium.Analytics.featureEvent('app.feature.blah');
```

You usually call the featureEvent method when the user has reached a particular screen or used a feature of the app that you want to make note of. When you later run Analytics Reports, you'll be able to see a count of how many people trigged that feature to be logged, whether that's going to a screen, or clicking a button, or anything that can generate an event. This gives you an easy way to record when a particular feature of your app was used, and can come in handy when you are trying to decide which features to enhance, maintain, or perhaps, do away with.

Although the Titanium.Analytics API is small, it can bring huge value to your application by helping you find out who is using your app, where they are using it, and what features people use most.

Titanium.Android

This is the top-level Android module.

Titanium.Android.currentActivity

In almost all cases, an activity is associated with a window. Activities are central to Android's Back button navigation. The Back button closes the current activity and returns to whatever activity was open previously.

In Titanium, you can create either "lightweight" or a "heavyweight" windows, as described on the Titanium.UI.Window reference page. A heavyweight window creates a new Activity. A lightweight window runs inside the same activity as the code that created it.

Titanium.Android.Calendar

This namespace can retrieve information about existing events and create new events. However, modifying or deleting existing events is not yet supported. Additionally, recurring events are not yet supported. The following code prints the names of all of your calendars known to Android, then prints the names of calendars that the user has selected in the native Android calendar application:

```
function showCalendars(calendars) {
    for (var i = 0; i < calendars.length; i++) {
        Ti.API.info(calendars[i].name);
    }
}

Ti.API.info('ALL CALENDARS:');
showCalendars(Ti.Android.Calendar.allCalendars);
Ti.API.info('SELECTABLE CALENDARS:');
showCalendars(Ti.Android.Calendar.selectableCalendars);
```

The list of calendars returned might be a subset of all the user's calendars, because the device may know about more calendars—for example, via the user's Google account—that the user has not selected inside the calendar app.

Titanium.Android.NotificationManager

This is a thin wrapper around the Android `NotificationManager` class. Notifications on Android and iOS allow one part of an application to notify another. Some simple code to create a notification and then show it on Android is as follows:

```
var win = Titanium.UI.createWindow({
    title: 'Test',
    backgroundColor: '#fff'
});
win.open();
var intent = Ti.Android.createIntent({
    action: Ti.Android.ACTION_DIAL,
    data: 'tel:123'
});
```

```
var note = Ti.Android.NotificationManager.createNotification({
    tickerText: 'This is a notification',
    number: 1,
    contentTitle: 'Notification',
    contentText: 'Something interesting in the background',
    contentIntent: intent
});
Ti.Android.NotificationManager.notify(1,note);
```

This code made use of an intent, an Android-specific concept. An intent is more or less a handle to the current process. In iOS this is never really needed, because on iOS each app is a sandboxed private app that doesn't know about anything else. Android is designed with more flexibility, so there are situations, such as with notifications, that the system needs to know what app (i.e., intent) sent some information to the operating system. Since a notification can come from any app running on the device, the intent is passed in so the overall Android OS knows what app sent it in when it shows it on the status bar.

Titanium.App

This exposes a number of properties set in the *tiapp.xml* file. Three of these properties must be specified when the application is created: the application's name, ID, and URL. Although most values may be changed by editing the *tiapp.xml* file after creating the project, the ID is automatically generated and should not be changed.

The App ID is the same as the Bundle ID for iOS apps and can have a significant effect on your app if you change it. Things like Push Notifications and In-App purchases all drive off the Bundle ID. If you change this after setting up those features, you can easily disable them.

Titanium.App.Android

This is used to access Android application resources.

Titanium.App.iOS

This includes facilities to create and manage local notifications and background services on iOS devices. Local notifications are a way for an application that is not running in the foreground to let users know that it has information for them. When invoked, a notification is displayed containing a Close button to dismiss it and a customizable View button to bring the application into the foreground. Also, notifications can be configured to set an application icon badge, to show the number of pending notifications, and to generate a sound.

Titanium.App.Properties

This stores application-related data in property/value pairs that persist beyond application sessions and device power cycles. The following code samples show how to store a string in the `Properties` object and print it out:

```
Ti.App.Properties.setString('givenName','Paul');
Ti.API.info('The value of the givenName property is: ' +
            Ti.App.Properties.get- String('givenName'));

var props = Ti.App.Properties.listProperties();

for (var i=0 ; i<props.length; i++){
   var value = Ti.App.Properties.getString(props[i]);
   Ti.API.info(props[i] + ' = ' + value);
}
```

Titanium.Codec

This is a module for translating between primitive types and raw byte streams. The Codec module can be used for encoding strings and numbers into Buffer objects, and decoding primitive types from buffers. This is usually not needed for things like reading from and writing to files, as these are covered by other functions.

One area where Codecs could be used is when doing advanced network operations, such as doing direct socket communications or other lower-level modes of network operations.

Titanium.Contacts

This is the top-level Contacts namespace, used to access the device's address book. Contacts in Android are read-only in Titanium.

Titanium.Database

This creates and accesses the SQLite database on an Android or iOS device.

SQLite databases can really be a boon to an app with moderate database needs. The sweet spot for these types of databases are apps that need to present table-based data in a variety of different ways. By using a simple "order by" in a SQL statement, you can easily pull the same data out ordered appropriately to the context that the data is being used.

Titanium.Facebook

This connects your application with Facebook. The module supports:

- Logging in to Facebook and authorizing your application
- Making requests through the Facebook Graph API
- Making requests through the legacy Facebook REST API
- Posting Facebook dialogs

The following code shows how to log into Facebook:

```
Ti.Facebook.appid = '[YOUR APPID]';
Ti.Facebook.permissions = ['publish_stream']; // Permissions your app needs
Ti.Facebook.addEventListener('login', function(e) {
    if (e.success) {
        alert('Logged In');
    } else if (e.error) {
        alert(e.error);
    } else if (e.cancelled) {
        alert("Canceled");
    }
});
Ti.Facebook.authorize();
```

Titanium.Filesystem

This accesses files and directories on the device.

Titanium.Geolocation

This accesses the device location.

Titanium.Gesture

This handles user gestures, such as taps and swipes.

Titanium.Locale

This works with localization information on the device, such as strings that represent dates and currency. The Locale namespace provides locale-specific strings that can be referenced at runtime. Additionally, the module contains a few methods and properties for querying the device's locale information.

Titanium.Map

This creates maps for use in an app. The following sample code creates a map with a pin on one site, and handles a user click. The click event is generated when the user taps the map or the annotation (pin):

```
var mountainView = Titanium.Map.createAnnotation({
    latitude:37.390749,
    longitude:-122.081651,
    title:"Appcelerator Headquarters",
    subtitle:'Mountain View, CA',
    pincolor:Titanium.Map.ANNOTATION_RED,
    animate:true,
    leftButton: '../images/appcelerator_small.png',
    myid:1 // Custom property to uniquely identify this annotation.
});

var mapview = Titanium.Map.createView({
    mapType: Titanium.Map.STANDARD_TYPE,
    region: {latitude:33.74511, longitude:-84.38993,
            latitudeDelta:0.01, longitudeDelta:0.01},
    animate:true,
    regionFit:true,
    userLocation:true,
    annotations:[mountainView]
});

mapview.addEventListener('click',
function(evt) {
    Ti.API.info("Annotation " + evt.title +
        " clicked, id: " + evt.annotation.myid);
    // Check for all of the possible names that clicksouce
    // can report for the left button/view.
    if (evt.clicksource == 'leftButton' || evt.clicksource == 'leftPane' ||
        evt.clicksource == 'leftView') {
        Ti.API.info("Annotation " + evt.title + ", left button clicked.");
    }
});
```

The click event is a fairly multi-purpose event on a MapView. This is where the click source property becomes invaluable. It lets you know whether the user was clicking on the map that contains the pin, the pin itself, or the right button on the annotation label when it pops up in response to a tap.

The click event is generated when the user taps on the map itself or an annotation on the map. By inspecting the evt.clicksource, as in the previous code, you can see what element of the map the user tapped to generate the click event. Some of the possible sources are the map itself, an annotation on the map, or some of the elements associated with the annotation. For instance, on iOS, when you tap the annotation, a small popover is presented with some details about the annotation. When you tap on elements contained in the popover, the click event is generated for those as well.

Titanium.Media

This accesses the device's media-related functionality, such as playing audio or recording video. It includes an Android-specific namespace (`Titanium.Media.Android`) for just two Android-specific functions, namely `scanMediaFiles()` and `setSystemWallpaper()`. All the other functions are platform independent.

If you're asking yourself where the corresponding iOS functions are, they don't exist. There is always the chance to have a native function that is available on one platform and not on another one, and this is an example of just that. Instead of hiding the function that exists on Android, Appcelerator exposed it, but in a namespace that gives you a clue that it only exists on one platform and not across multiple ones.

Titanium.Network

This handles network events, such as downloads.

Titanium.Network.Socket

This is a relatively low-level networking activity, used for creating and communicating over sockets.

Titanium.Platform

This accesses the device's platform-related functionality. The functions in this namespace relate to specifics regarding the platform that the app is running on, while still being portable across multiple platforms. These functions include things like `batteryState`, `osname`, and other properties that relate to the platform the app is running on.

Titanium.Stream

This module provides a set of methods for interacting with `IOStream` objects, including asynchronous versions of the read and write methods offered by all stream objects. These methods should be used in any place where reading from or writing to a stream might block.

Titanium.UI

This is responsible for native user-interface components and interaction inside Titanium. The goal of the UI module is to provide a native experience along with native performance by compiling JavaScript code into its native counterparts.

Titanium.UI.Android

This includes all the Android-specific UI capabilities. All properties, methods, and events in this namespace will work only on Android devices.

Titanium.UI.Clipboard

This accesses the clipboard, where data is stored during cut and copy operations:

```
Copying text to the clipboard
copyButton.addEventListener('click', function() {
    Ti.UI.Clipboard.setText(data.url);
});
Pasting text from the clipboard
if (Ti.UI.Clipboard.hasText()) {
    doSomethingWith(Ti.UI.Clipboard.getText());
} else {
    alert('Hey there was no text.');
}
```

Titanium.UI.iOS

This includes all the Apple iOS-specific UI capabilities. All properties, methods, and events in this namespace will work only on iOS devices. It features constants, especially near the top of the namespace, for options that are used by methods farther down in the namespace.

Titanium.UI.iPad

This has iPad-specific UI capabilities. All properties, methods, and events in this namespace work only on Apple's iPad devices. To use these features properly, please review the iPad Human Interface Guidelines (*http://developer.apple.com/iphone/library/docu mentation/General/Conceptual/iPadHIG/Introduction/Introduction.html*).

Titanium.UI.iPhone

This has iPhone-specific UI capabilities. All properties, methods, and events in this namespace work on both iPhone and iPad devices.

Titanium.UI.MobileWeb

These are UI capabilities specific to Mobile Web. All events, methods, and properties in this namespace will work only on the browser version of your app.

Titanium.Utils

This contains methods that are often useful when building applications. For example, I wrote an app in Titanium that allowed you to interact with servers of an online game. There was a salt parameter that was basically a second level of security that you passed in with each API call.

The actual value of the salt parameter was set on the server and on the mobile app. To help keep the salt value confidential, it was run through a sha256 hash and the resulting hash was then sent to the server. Using the sha256 function in the Ti.Utils namespace made it easy to generate this hash and include it with the API call.

Titanium.XML

These methods parse and process XML-based content.

Titanium.Yahoo

This accesses Yahoo-related API services.

About the Author

John Anderson always tells people that he feels like computers picked him, and not the other way around. While in grade school he walked into a Radio Shack, got his first look at a TRS-80, and fell in love. From that point on, computers and programming was the main focus in his life. All he could afford was the manual, so that's what he bought and started learning about programming. He has stayed with that model of learning about new technologies by getting a good book and learning about a new topic. He's been programming computers for about 20 years now, starting as a Customer Support Rep, getting his first programming job, and working his way up. When the Internet got popular, he jumped onto that as the Next Big Thing and his career built on that for over 10 years. A couple years ago when a similar phenomenon was happening in Mobile, he again took to the books and started building his own mobile apps and immersing himself in all things mobile. He has apps in Apple's App Store and the Android Marketplace, some of which were done with Titanium.

Colophon

The animal on the cover of *Appcelerator Titanium: Up and Running* is a golden lion tamarin (*Leontopithecus rosalia*).

The cover image is from Meyers Kleines *Lexikon*. The cover font is Adobe ITC Garamond. The text font is Adobe Minion Pro; the heading font is Adobe Myriad Condensed; and the code font is Dalton Maag's Ubuntu Mono.

Have it your way.

Get even more for your money.

Join the O'Reilly Community, and register the O'Reilly books you own. It's free, and you'll get:

- $4.99 ebook upgrade offer
- 40% upgrade offer on O'Reilly print books
- Membership discounts on books and events
- Free lifetime updates to ebooks and videos
- Multiple ebook formats, DRM FREE
- Participation in the O'Reilly community
- Newsletters
- Account management
- 100% Satisfaction Guarantee

Signing up is easy:

1. Go to: oreilly.com/go/register
2. Create an O'Reilly login.
3. Provide your address.
4. Register your books.

Note: English-language books only

To order books online:
oreilly.com/store

For questions about products or an order:
orders@oreilly.com

To sign up to get topic-specific email announcements and/or news about upcoming books, conferences, special offers, and new technologies:
elists@oreilly.com

For technical questions about book content:
booktech@oreilly.com

To submit new book proposals to our editors:
proposals@oreilly.com

O'Reilly books are available in multiple DRM-free ebook formats. For more information:
oreilly.com/ebooks

O'REILLY®

Spreading the knowledge of innovators   oreilly.com

Lightning Source UK Ltd.
Milton Keynes UK
UKOW07f1514120417
298947UK00001B/56/P